Brokeback Mountain

American Indies

Series Editors: Gary Needham and Yannis Tzioumakis

Brokeback Mountain

Gary Needham

Edinburgh University Press

Illustrations appear courtesy of the following copyright holders:
Focus Features (Figures 1, 2, 6–11); United Artists/MGM (Figure 3);
AMG (Figure 4); Kino Video (Figure 5)

Edinburgh University Press Ltd
22 George Square, Edinburgh

www.euppublishing.com

Reprinted 2010

Typeset in 11/13pt Monotype Baskerville by
Servis Filmsetting Ltd, Stockport, Cheshire, and
printed and bound by CPI Antony Rowe, Chippenham
and Eastbourne

A CIP record for this book is available from the British Library

ISBN 978 0 7486 3382 1 (hardback)
ISBN 978 0 7486 3383 8 (paperback)

Contents

Series Preface

In recent years American independent cinema has not only become the focus of significant scholarly attention but as a category of film it has shifted from a marginal to a central position within American cinema – a shift that can be also detected in the emergence of the label 'indie' cinema as opposed to independent cinema. The popularisation of this 'indie' brand of filmmaking began in the 1990s with the commercial success of the Sundance Film Festival and of specialty distributor Miramax Films, as well as the introduction of DVD, which made independent films more readily available as well as profitable for the first time. At the same time, film studies started developing courses that distinguished American independent cinema from mainstream Hollywood, treating it as a separate object of study and a distinct discursive category.

Despite the surge in interest in independent cinema, a surge that involved the publication of at least twenty books and edited collections alongside a much larger number of articles on various aspects of independent cinema, especially about the post-1980 era, the field – as it has developed – still remains greatly under-researched in relation to the changes of the past twenty years that define the shift from independent to 'indie' cinema. This is partly because a multifaceted phenomenon such as American independent cinema, the history of which is as long and complex as the history of mainstream Hollywood, has yet to be adequately and satisfactorily documented. In this respect, academic film criticism is still in great need to account for the plethora of shapes, forms and guises that American independent cinema has manifested itself in. This is certainly not an easy task given that independent film has, indeed, taken a wide variety of forms at different historical trajectories and has been influenced by a hugely diverse range of factors.

It is with this problem in mind that 'American Indies' was conceived by its editors. While the history of American independent cinema is still being written with more studies already set to be published in the forthcoming years, and while journal articles are enhancing our understanding of more focused aspects of independent filmmaking, the 'American Indies' series has been created to provide the necessary space to explore and engage with specific examples of American 'indie' films in a great depth. Through this format, 'American Indies' aims to encourage an examination of both the 'indie' text and its contexts, of understanding how 'indie' films operate within a particular filmmaking practice but also how 'indies' have been shaping a new formation of American cinema. In this respect, 'American Indies' provides the space for a detailed examination of industrial, economic and institutional concerns alongside the more usual formal and aesthetic considerations that have historically characterised critical approaches of independent films. 'American Indies' is a series of comprehensive studies of carefully selected examples of recent films that reveal in great detail the many sides of the phenomenon of the recently emerged American 'indie' cinema.

As the first book series to explore and define this aspect of American cinema, 'American Indies' has had the extremely difficult task of producing a comprehensive set of criteria that informs its selection of titles. Given the vastness of the field, we have made several editorial decisions in order to produce a coherent definition of this new phase of American independent cinema. The first such choice was to concentrate on recent examples of independent cinema. Although the word 'recent' has often been used to include films made in the post-1980 period, as editors we decided that the cut-off point for films to be included in this series would be the year 1996. This was an extremely significant year in the independent film sector, 'the year of the independents' as was triumphantly proclaimed by the *Los Angeles Business Journal* in February 1997, for a number of reasons. Arguably, the most significant of these reasons was the dynamic entrance in the film market of Fox Searchlight, a new type of a specialty film division created by 20th Century Fox in 1995 with the explicit intention of claiming a piece of the increasingly large independent film market pie. Fox Searchlight would achieve this objective through the production and distribution of films that followed many of the conventions of independent film as those were established after the success of *sex, lies and videotape* in 1989. These conventions had since then started being popularised by a number of films produced and distributed by Miramax Films, an independent company that was taken over by

Disney after the phenomenal box office success of several of its films at approximately the same time as 20th Century Fox was establishing its specialty division.

The now direct involvement of entertainment conglomerates like Disney and Fox in the independent film sector had far-reaching effects. Arguably, the most important of these was that the label 'independent', which for critics and the cinema going public (wrongly) signified economic independence from major film companies like Disney, Fox, Paramount, Universal, etc., obviously ceased to convey this meaning. Instead, critics and public alike started using increasingly the label 'indie' which suggested a particular type of film that adhered to a set of conventions as well as a transformed independent cinema sector that was now driven by specialty companies, most of them subsidiaries of major entertainment conglomerates. It is this form of 'independent' cinema that has produced some of the most interesting films to come out of American cinema in recent years that 'American Indies' has set out to explore in great depth and which explains our selection of the label 'indies' instead of independents.

We hope readers will enjoy the series
Gary Needham and Yannis Tzioumakis
American Indies Series Editors

Acknowledgements

There are many people to thank who supported, discussed and put up with my obsession with *Brokeback Mountain*. They are Karen Boyle, Kay Dickinson, Dimitris Eleftheriotis, Amelie Hastie, Joanne Hollows, Chris Holmlund, Sian Lincoln, Claire Molloy, Liz Morrish, Martin O'Shaughnessy, Lydia Papadimtriou, Denis Provencher, Christopher Pullen, Amy Villarejo, Dave Woods and Greg Woods. A special thanks to Glyn Davis, co-conspirator in all things queer, and Belen Vidal, both of whom read chapter drafts and were able to make many useful suggestions. Jackie Jones, thanks for your patience. This book would not be what it is without the support and friendship of Yannis Tzioumakis. We conceived of the series together and few will ever know how much of this particular book was made possible by him. I can't thank him enough. And finally, to David Oswald, for love and support, thanks for not quitting.

Brokeback Mountain is dedicated to Eve Kosofsky Sedgwick (1950–2009).

Introduction: Brokaholics Anonymous

My name is Gary and I'm a Brokaholic! I admit that this book was initially conceived out of an obsession with the film and for that it has been a hard book to write. When I told film studies colleagues that I was both overly affected by the material and intending to write about the film many took a sharp intake of breath as if to suggest that it was a terrible idea. I think the assumption here is that one is going to work out one's 'issues' through scholarship and that objectivity is going to be unquestionably compromised. However, this was not the response of colleagues from the queer studies community. As a matter of fact I was actively encouraged to undertake this project, since doing queer work is in itself a venture that has no fear of emotions, affects, subjective exploration and analysis. Emotional involvement apparently places theoretical objectivity on shaky ground but I would defend feeling as intrinsic not only to the experience of being queer,[1] but also to the conduct of queer work.

Before I entered the theatre in January of 2006 for the first of many repeat viewings of *Brokeback Mountain* that month, I had few expectations that the film was going to be anything special. Prior to the film's release I was not convinced by the critical praise of the film's queer credentials and B. Ruby Rich's hyperbole that this was a going to be a film that would change our perception of cinema and film history let alone explode with new possibilities to rethink independent cinema, genre and gay spectatorship.[2] I anticipated *Brokeback Mountain* being a good film, since Ang Lee is consistently dependable in terms of his craft, but I did not expect *Brokeback Mountain* to have a profoundly affective emotional impact. For a film about the closet and homosexual desire *Brokeback Mountain* did a good job in making apparent the often closeted and closeting nature of cinemagoing for gay and lesbian spectators. *Brokeback Mountain* contributes to thinking about the closet not only through the film's dramatisation of the closet, but in terms of how much one is compelled to reveal, as a gay spectator or otherwise – to respond with tears, to even ask for a ticket – in the potentially unsafe and homophobic spaces of the multiplex cinema. It is important to point out that Focus Features and the indie film have helped bridge the exhibition gap between multiplex and art house. No matter how out and proud one claims to be, it is difficult to escape the ingrained feelings of shame, paranoia and self-surveillance around homosexuality that constitute both its past and its present, linking the characters of Ennis and Jack to the gay and lesbian spectators in the auditorium.

Brokeback Mountain is an indie film but it is also a queer film. Labelling it queer is a way of suggesting that it unsettles conventions, common sense assumptions and concepts of what is normal and normative. The queerness of *Brokeback Mountain* takes account of a range of ways of thinking queerly about the text and not just in relation to sexuality; for example, this book is also about the queering of film genre. It is important to consider that queer is antagonistic to normal or normative, which means that the opposite of queer is not necessarily straight or heterosexual as one might think. The queer issues may seem most obvious in relation to the simple fact that the film is of about two closeted homosexual men but perhaps queerness is less obvious when one considers film form, such as the editing patterns discussed in Chapter 4, or affect as discussed in Chapter 3, for these often do not appear really to be about sexuality at all.

Queer, homosexual and gay are not all the same thing but at times it may seem that I am using the terms interchangeably or inconsistently. A question of style has certainly been involved and when I have made certain choices it might also be to avoid boring the reader with repetition. The general tendency I adopt in this book is that queer is used as a critical term or category that incorporates in its meaning an unsettling or dismantling of normativity in all its manifestations, especially as those relate to common sense assumptions about gender and sexuality. I use gay most often to refer to gay men and gay identity and culture as separate from straight men and lesbians. My most common use of homosexuality is merely to indicate same sex desire and contact. There is slippage between terms but I have tried for the most part to avoid it. As characters I would consider Jack Twist and Ennis del Mar to be homosexual rather than gay. *Brokeback Mountain* as a text is queer (as an adjective) but it also queers (as a verb) the genres of the Western and the melodrama.

Queer theory is a privileged framework in this book, for it is difficult to imagine making sense of *Brokeback Mountain* without it, and through it film studies and film genre itself can be invigorated. I also hope that my discussion, drawn from a range of queer thought and scholarship from canonical works to more recent arguments, demonstrates the ongoing relevance of queer theory for cinema. I consider this book to be a dialogue between film studies and queer theory, informed by the objective and subjective considerations of each discipline, which will examine why *Brokeback Mountain* is both an important work of cinema and independent film (following film studies) and an important political and cultural experience (following queer studies). It would also seem that this relationship between film studies and queer theory is one that is fostered through *Brokeback Mountain*'s status as an independent film with links to the New Queer Cinema of the early 1990s and more generally with the American independent cinema scene of the 1990s.

Brokeback Mountain as an Independent Film

As a volume in the series 'American Indies', *Brokeback Mountain* is well placed to contribute to the study of American independent film in the twenty-first century. It is in Chapter 1 that I will discuss the industrial location of *Brokeback Mountain*. Specifically, the chapter will examine the film as one of the key productions in the short history of Universal's specialty division, Focus Features. That company represents one of the most successful examples of what Yannis Tzioumakis has termed 'the third wave of the classics divisions',[3] a recent move within the major entertainment conglomerates to establish a new brand of subsidiaries that would dominate more effectively the American independent film market than previous organisations like Sony Pictures Classics and Fine Line Features. By the time of Focus Features' establishment in 2002, that market had become extremely lucrative, especially after the incredible commercial success of independent films such as *The Blair Witch Project* (Sanchez and Myrick, 1999) and *My Big Fat Greek Wedding* (J. Zwick, 2002), which recorded $140 million and $242 million respectively at the North American box office and convinced the majors that independent films can indeed achieve commercial success that is usually associated with major blockbuster productions. The chapter will chart the often convoluted history of the company, explore its links and connections with a number of other key players in the sector of the time (especially USA Films and Good Machine) and argue that its success has been largely due to its association with a particular brand of quality independent filmmaking that has been well-received by public and critics alike: *Far from Heaven* (Haynes, 2002); *Lost in Translation* (S. Coppola, 2003); *21 Grams* (Iñárritu, 2003); *Eternal Sunshine of the Spotless Mind* (Gondry, 2004); *Brick* (R. Johnson, 2005); *Broken Flowers* (Jarmusch, 2005); *Into the Wild* (Penn, 2007); *Milk* (Van Sant, 2008); and of course *Brokeback Mountain*. These (now classic) Focus Features indie films have also been supplemented by a substantial number of quality non-US films that the company distributed as part of its brand strategy over the years: *The Pianist* (Polanski, 2002); *Swimming Pool* (Ozon, 2003); *Diarios de motocicleta* [*The Motorcycle Diaries*] (Salles, 2004); *The Constant Gardener* (Meirelles, 2005); *Atonement* (J. Wright, 2007).

Equally importantly, the chapter will also examine Focus Features and *Brokeback Mountain* as quintessential examples of a shift in American independent cinema that produced a new mode of filmmaking that has been labelled, often controversially, 'indie cinema'. Given the hefty budget for the film (estimated at $14 million) and the presence of an entertainment conglomerate's subsidiary in the double role of producer and distributor,[4] the chapter questions the usefulness of the term 'independent' in any critical approaches of contemporary (post mid-1990s) American cinema. Instead, it argues for the use of the term 'indie' as a distinct category of filmmaking within the greater American independent cinema landscape, a category that sits comfortably with the move of the entertainment conglomerates to the independent market, the exponential growth of production and distribution budgets, the presence of stars (and often superstars) in the credits, the advertising of films of such designation in malls, their release in thousands of screens and other such developments. The chapter will discuss these developments in some detail and will suggest that Focus Features is the paradigmatic 'indie' company within this particular environment and that *Brokeback Mountain* benefited from its association with this company from inception.

Brokeback Mountain as a Genre Film

One of the most contested and risible issues surrounding *Brokeback Mountain* was the film's generic status as a Western. In part, this was because the Western has close ties with American history and national mythology as well as links with certain forms of normative and hegemonic masculinity, often idealised as stoic, conservative and, most of all, 'straight'. With the film questioning directly all these staples of masculinity, Chapter 2 sets out to provide a lengthy exploration and validation of *Brokeback Mountain* as a Western. To achieve these objectives this chapter is structured in two sections. In the first section, *Brokeback Mountain* is examined as a Western text with an emphasis on how it relates to and diverges from the core meaning of the Western as a Hollywood film genre, especially as the latter has been debated and understood in film studies. Following this contextualisation, the rest of the first section will utilise queer theory in order to demonstrate how the Western film genre can be rethought in alternative ways. The second part of the chapter positions *Brokeback Mountain* within a wider historical net concerning the links between the Western and homosexuality, a net that dates back to classical Westerns such as *Red River* (Hawks, 1948) and extends to underground films such as Andy Warhol's *Horse* (1965). What yokes both sections is not just *Brokeback Mountain* the film, but a wider set of questions and issues that allows sexual politics and queerness to be articulated in relation to one of American cinema's most precious and enduring film genres. As the chapter will demonstrate, it is a central tenet of contemporary independent films like *Brokeback* Mountain to be able to experiment with, and ultimately stretch, the meaning of what constitutes genre in American cinema.

Chapter 3 continues its exploration of questions of genre with an analysis of *Brokeback Mountain*'s relationship to melodrama. As a cultural form, melodrama is often considered to be a way of perceiving the world in response to specific social and political pressures. Therefore, one can propose that *Brokeback Mountain* as a melodramatic form of film is importantly placed to utilise the genre in order to explore ongoing problems of the closet and homophobia in contemporary US gay and lesbian social, cultural and political life. Chapter 3 requires one to touch upon theories of melodrama as developed in film studies but also, and necessarily, queer theory, which has influenced my approach to the Western in Chapter 2. Melodrama would seem to respond well to queer theory's recent turn to a politics of negative feeling. As I will argue, *Brokeback Mountain*'s real power stems from the way it mobilises melodrama and queer negative feeling, which together produce an affective and emotionally queer film experience. *Brokeback Mountain* is all about pathos and the feelings of pity and powerlessness it cultivates for the spectator. Powerlessness, emotional vulnerability and a constant waiting are relentlessly underscored by the melodramatic structures of storytelling and create an experience of passivity and helplessness that tends to be overwhelming.

The importance of *Brokeback Mountain* is that it refuses to portray homosexuality as anything but a difficult and emotive subject and melodrama is one means through which to do this. *Brokeback Mountain* demands that we accept that homosexuality is still impossible for many. That homosexuality is still permeated by tragedy and melancholia, and that it has a history that is still unresolved and needful of being properly negotiated in the present. Therefore, the politicisation of emotion and affect in relation to the closet and homophobia, disproportionate relations between past and present, character and spectator, are what make *Brokeback Mountain* meaningful as a queer melodrama.

Brokeback Mountain and Spectatorship

Spectatorship is a theme that runs through this book but it becomes a central focus in Chapter 4 where I consider a sequence of shots in *Brokeback Mountain* and their relationship to gay spectatorship. This chapter is concerned with interrelationships between gay male cruising, spectatorship and editing and the argument I propose is based around a shot/reverse shot structure. These shots refer to Jack and Ennis's first encounter and the way they are presented may strike a chord of recognition with the gay spectator because it resembles cruising. This opening scene privileges the knowledge of the gay spectator as a cultural viewer who identifies the silent codes of exchange between two homosexual men. In this respect, this is not simply a scene of spatial continuity and I argue instead that editing confirms the gay spectator's position in relation to the film, and the men's relationship, through its structural analogy with cruising.

As a formal system, editing is different from narrative yet it contributes to the overall meanings generated by the film in terms of how shot relations position us to see narrative events and understand Jack and Ennis's relationship. This is most evident in how their desire for one another and the history of their relationship is, I will argue, in part told through shot relations.

Conclusion

Each of the four chapters in this book could stand alone in situating *Brokeback Mountain* in relation to specific frameworks and debates: indie cinema; the Western; the melodrama; gay spectatorship and cruising.

They can be read in a linear fashion but also read in isolation. What links them together, other than the film itself, is *Brokeback Mountain*'s status as a key indie feature and the way that fosters a dialogue between film studies and queer theory and the myriad ways *Brokeback Mountain* seems to circulate as both a mainstream (must see cultural phenomenon) and an alternative (independent, queer) film. *Brokeback Mountain*'s reception, whether it was the first reports from film festivals, coverage in gay lifestyle magazines and national newspapers, the forums dedicated to the film, the way it was received at the 2006 Oscars, all these contributed to an incredibly rich source of zeitgeist buzz. This is an important part of *Brokeback Mountain*'s story that Harry Benshoff has begun to shed some light on.[5] For such an important film this book has a lot to live up to. As a volume in the *American Indies* series this book is also my reception of the film.

1. The Indie in Focus

Introduction

The presence of *Brokeback Mountain* at awards and throughout popular culture was a testament to the film and its producer-distributor, Focus Features, who generated an enormous amount of critical buzz, acclaim and widespread exposure. *Brokeback Mountain*'s success as a modest crossover hit was indicative of a new climate for independent cinema, one that frequently positions independent films between the mainstream successes associated with studio pictures and the cultural capital and edginess of the independent feature. *Brokeback Mountain* entered the mainstream consciousness like no other widely distributed gay-themed independent film before it and since; *Milk* (Gus Van Sant, 2008) became a critical and commercial success but did not reproduce the buzz and revenue that accompanied *Brokeback Mountain*. *Brokeback Mountain*'s unexpected media visibility and cultural presence (through marketing, awards, good box office returns, water-cooler chit-chat, gossip and countless pop culture references) gesture towards a different kind of independent film, one far removed from what was understood by the term 'independent film' in the previous two decades. *Brokeback Mountain*'s success was also unusual for a film with such widely publicised gay leanings, especially since it was often positioned critically in relation to the Western genre. On the other hand, *Brokeback Mountain*'s cultural momentum chimes with many other critically and commercially successful independent films, which have complicated considerably in recent years the very meanings attached to the terms 'independent film' and 'American independent cinema'.

Brokeback Mountain and Focus Features are representative of an emergent and ongoing paradigm shift in American independent cinema's self-definition that is indicated by a preference for the terms 'indie' and 'indiewood' as opposed to 'independent'. One of the aims of this chapter is to explore exactly what the 'indie' designation actually means from the point of view of company operations within an enlarged independent sector and how this affects institutional definitions of independent cinema. It is obvious that *Brokeback Mountain*'s aesthetic dimensions and narrative situations are axiomatic of the 'independent spirit'; that is easy to defend by the very fact of its gay content, languorous film style and the authorial presence of Ang Lee. However, when it comes to the nitty-gritty of defining *Brokeback Mountain* as an independent film – how the film becomes an instance of independent production and distribution – this is where quotation marks begin to appear around the terms 'independent' and 'indie'.

Independent vs Indie

In an era of media conglomeration, multinational acquisitions and industry synergies, the test of a film's independence becomes increasingly more difficult and complex and calls into question the validity of the term 'independent' as something that signifies a separateness and autonomy from the equally diffuse terms 'studio film' and 'mainstream cinema'. Attempting to homogenise American independent cinema, especially in opposition to the concepts of Hollywood and the mainstream, quickly leads to an obfuscating terrain in which the relationship between the indies and the studios is at times unclear (perhaps deliberately) and inseparable; hence the preference for the term indie as a specific designation for this necessary contemporary mapping of what might be characterised as 'the indie after the independent'. The indie is a type of film and a mode of production and distribution cushioned between the independent and the studio context, an industry hybrid in a state of indeterminate in-betweenness. As a context for *Brokeback Mountain* this chapter unpacks the concept of the indie by tracing the conceptual and paradigmatic shifts suggested in the transition from an independent cinema to an indie cinema primarily through an examination of Focus Features.

The indie film points to a new industrial organisation of independent cinema through the formation and ascendancy of the classics divisions, or studio speciality arms. Focus Features is the speciality arm of Universal. Focus Features and the eventual realisation of *Brokeback Mountain* are also the result of the ever changing and transitory nature of film production companies, distribution companies, a Hollywood major, and corporate media manoeuvring that chronicle the history of independent cinema since the 1990s. In relation to Focus Features, this history would include USA Films, Good Machine, Universal and their complicated corporate entanglement during a period of time that stretches from the mid-1990s to the early 2000s; their story is in part the narrative of how independent cinema became indie cinema.

Focus Features is the definitive indie company in the 2000s in the same way that Miramax once defined the 1990s independent landscape. In fact, a reductive account of the creation of Focus Features is to merely view it as Universal's attempt to usurp Miramax's hegemony in what is known as the independent sector or the specialty film market. In film industry and media trade papers Focus Features is always defined in business terms as a motion picture production, financing and world distribution company.[1] In addition to this, the business definitions also suggest that Focus Features provides art house film product for its parent company NBC Universal. NBC Universal was created out of the American television network NBC (National Broadcasting Company) and the Hollywood major Universal. At the time of writing NBC Universal is controlled and owned by two larger corporate entities with General Electric controlling 80 per cent of the company and with the media giant Vivendi controlling the remaining 20 per cent. This elaborate corporate structure certainly prompts one to ask just how independent Focus Features can really be when the company is a subsidiary of a much larger enterprise – not just a Hollywood studio's younger relative but one of the many small cogs in one business sector of a gigantic conglomerate empire. However, the answer to this question is never straightforward. This is because, on the one hand, independent cinema is not what it was in previous decades (independent of studios and conglomerates) while, on the other hand, Focus Features is autonomous to the extent that it can finance and distribute *Brokeback Mountain* without the parent company's permission, which is certainly not what one would consider a conventional studio film by any means.

The attendant questions of periodising independent cinema are arduous and contradictory, drawing upon longstanding, if not clearly articulated, tensions between two overlapping modes of definition: the mode of production versus the aesthetic and the ideological. The notion that one can tell an independent film from mainstream through style or politics remains central to independent cinema's pedestrian understanding as a cinematic experience that differs from the norm. As a matter of fact, indies like Fox Searchlight's *Juno* (Jason Reitman, 2007) try very hard to self-consciously inculcate the indie vibe for a general audience that is not especially attuned to the political, cultural and industrial nuances that have shaped Hollywood's other. *Juno* is a film that often feels forced in its attempt to cram as much alterity as is possible into ninety minutes. If abortion is the topic that gives *Juno* part of its edgy indie credibility then compared to the similarly themed Todd Solondz's *Palindromes* (2004), *Juno* is, for want of a better expression, indie-*lite*. Films like *Palindromes* could be the litmus test for audiences' tipping point and an indication of where an ideological and aesthetic demarcation can be drawn between the Fox Searchlight indie and the Wellspring Media distributed independent film.

Similarly, but on the other side of the production fence, a studio picture like Ang Lee's *Hulk* (2003) works in the opposite direction, namely, a Universal summer blockbuster with the complexities and rhythms of an independent film (like *Brokeback Mountain*, *Hulk* was also co-produced by the independent company Good Machine). In her book on Ang Lee, Whitney Crothers Dilley suggests that the 'narrative, tone and pacing that was neither big-budget blockbuster nor small-budget art house, [was] an awkward combination of the two', which serves as one possible explanation of the *Hulk*'s relatively poor box office performance (the film failed to even cover its $137 million price tag).[2]

The desire to pin down the meaning of independent cinema in terms of the ideological and the aesthetic, a question of art and authorship, can often be misguided as the perception of independence (again to take *Juno* as the example here) is also a matter of reception practices and the personal standpoints of both the industry and the audience. However, with the mode of production and industrial organisation as the primary focal points, one is dealing with what is at the very least assumed to be the facts of the matter plain and simple: how the film industry operates. As Yannis Tzioumakis outlines at the beginning of *American Independent Cinema: An Introduction*, New Line Cinema's *Lord of the Rings* trilogy (2001–3) is by all accounts an example of independent cinema, but there again, so is *Palindromes*.[3] How can one make sense of these films as independent under a rubric that tends to prioritise aesthetic and ideological definitions?

Tzioumakis goes on to suggest that we work with an instructive model of discursive complexity that 'expands and contracts when socially authorised institutions (filmmakers, industry practitioners, trade publications, academics, film critics and so on) contribute towards its definition'.[4] Thus Tzioumakis offers a Foucauldian tinged framework for grappling with the definitions of independent cinema at any given time; after all, how else can one group together under the same banner such disparate and polarised features as *Shakespeare in Love* (John Madden, 1998) and *Mysterious Skin* (Gregg Araki, 2004), let alone attempt to define and confer continuity in the shift from New Queer Cinema independents such as *Swoon* (Tom Kalin, 1992) and *Go Fish* (Rose Troche, 1994) to the sort of quasi-mainstream acceptance of indies like *Brokeback Mountain* and *Kissing Jessica Stein* (Charles Herman-Wurmfield, 2001)?

Focus Features Pre-history Snapshot: Good Machine and USA Films

The film production (and occasionally distribution) company Good Machine is where Focus Features begins, as this was where the ongoing creative relationship between Ang Lee and James Schamus commenced. Schamus and Ted Hope founded the New York based company in 1991 when both men were script readers at New Line Cinema. Through Good Machine they would go on to produce over forty films, many of them important independent features directed by a roster of independent film talents. Good Machine would also work with Christine Vachon's production company Killer Films, a relationship that still continues through Focus Features. The key feature of Good Machine, however, was that it functioned as an *indie film packager*, a company specialising in assembling the essential properties for a film (script, director, producer and finance) which they would either produce and distribute themselves or, in most instances, just produce and offer its distribution rights to a studio subsidiary. Good Machine was in a particularly strategic position to make an impact on the independent sector as they had managed to arrange *first look deals* for its packages with a number of established players, including, Fox, Miramax and importantly, Universal, the company where James Schamus would eventually end up as co-president of its Focus Features division.

The first important production overseen by Good Machine was *The Wedding Banquet* [*Xi Yan*] (1993), co produced with Taiwan's CMPC (Central Motion Pictures Corporation). *The Wedding Banquet* was also the second creative collaboration in story and script writing between Schamus and Ang Lee. Before Good Machine's production of *The*

Wedding Banquet, the company had handled the distribution of Ang Lee's first transnational feature-length picture *Pushing Hands* [*Tui Shuo*] (1992, Taiwan). According to Dilley, on the cusp of Good Machine's formation Schamus and Hope had originally caught Lee's New York University graduation film *A Fine Line*.[5] *The Wedding Banquet* came at the right moment riding the wave of both Asian-American Cinema and New Queer Cinema. Good Machine would also co-produce Todd Haynes's third film *[safe]* (1995) but it should be noted that they also rejected the edgier queer film *Go Fish*.[6]

The Wedding Banquet became a considerable hit at the US box office with $6,933,459, in an era before *Pulp Fiction* (Tarantino, 1994) and Ang Lee's own *Crouching Tiger, Hidden Dragon* [*Wo hu cang long*] (2000) redefined irreversibly the box office potential for independent, and non-US, art films. *The Wedding Banquet* would also net $30 million globally,[7] but it was the film's critical success, that far outweighed its financial returns, that allowed Ang Lee to be established as a new auteur of the 1990s. Lee would go on to direct *Eat Drink Man Woman* [*Yin shin an nu*] (1994, US/Taiwan), *The Ice Storm* (1997), *Ride With the Devil* (1999), *Crouching Tiger, Hidden Dragon*, *Hulk*, and *Brokeback Mountain*, all of which were either produced, co-produced or attached in some way to the Good Machine brand. While Good Machine's name still appears in the credits of *Brokeback Mountain*, by that time the company had been acquired by Universal (2002), co-founder Ted Hope had departed and James Schamus had been appointed co-president of Focus Features along with David Linde. Table 1 provides a list of all Good Machine's productions.

USA Films is a slightly different story from Good Machine as the company was more focused on its role as a distributor rather than a hyphenate producer-distributor. USA Films distributed forty-six titles during its lifespan as a theatrical distributor from 1999 to 2003 in comparison to only eight company productions between 2000 and 2003.[8] USA Films was run by Scott Greenstein (the former co-president of October films) and was viewed by the trade press as a less stable company than Good Machine with *Variety* proclaiming in 2000 that 'mega-indie' USA Films had 'deep pockets', 'flashy Logos' and 'high-power execs' before going on to question in the same line the company's position in the market.[9] Indeed, the same *Variety* article was rife with rhetorical statements, positing USA Films as 'an enigma' and asking 'what USA's game plan [is]'.[10] Nonetheless, the company's short history

Table 1 Good Machine productions

Film	Year	Director
Keep it For Yourself	1991	Claire Denis
Chicken Delight (short feature)	1991	Adam Isidore
The Maid (produced for television)	1991	Ian Toynton
The Wedding Banquet	1993	Ang Lee
River of Grass	1994	Kelly Reichhardt
What Happened was . . .	1994	Tom Noonan
Roy Cohn / Jack Smith	1994	Jill Godmilow
[safe]	1995	Todd Haynes
Walking and Talking	1996	Nicole Holofcener
She's the One	1996	Edward Burns
Arresting Gena	1996	Hannah Weyer
The Ice Storm	1997	Ang Lee
Office Killer	1997	Cindy Sherman
The Myth of Fingerprints	1997	Bart Freundlich
The Sticky Fingers of Time	1997	Hilary Brougher
Love God	1997	Frank Grow
Wonderland	1997	John O'Hagan
Xiu Xiu: The Sent Down Girl	1998	Joan Chen
No Looking Back	1998	Edward Burns
Happiness	1998	Todd Solondz
Luminous Motion	1998	Bette Gordon
Annabelle (short feature)	1999	Brian Champeau
Trick	1999	Jim Fall
The Lifestyle	1999	David Schisgall
Ride With the Devil	1999	Ang Lee
The Tao of Steve	2000	Jenniphr Goodman
The King is Alive	2000	uncredited (Dogme)
Crouching Tiger, Hidden Dragon	2000	Ang Lee
In the Bedroom	2001	Todd Field
The Devil's Backbone	2001	Guillermo del Toro
Storytelling	2001	Todd Solondz
The Man Who Wasn't There	2001	Joel Cohen
Human Nature	2001	Michel Gondry
Lovely and Amazing	2001	Nicole Holofcener
Buffalo Soldiers	2001	Gregor Jordan
The Laramie Project	2002	Moisés Kaufman
Talk to Her	2002	Pedro Almodóvar
Laurel Canyon	2002	Lisa Cholodenko
Auto Focus	2002	Paul Schrader
They	2002	Robert Harmon
Adaptation	2002	Spike Jonze

Table 1 (continued)

Film	Year	Director
American Splendor	2003	Shari S. Berman and Rob Pulcini
Hulk	2003	Ang Lee
*The Door in the Floor**	2004	Tod Williams
Promise	2004	K. Busler and W. J. Rooker
*Brokeback Mountain**	2006	Ang Lee

*   Co-produced and distributed by Focus Features[11]

is an important component in the eventual formation of Focus Features that many had assumed Scott Greenstein was going to head.

USA Films was tied to a few high profile auteur-star-driven independent films during this period and is notable for being the co-producer of *Traffic* (Soderbergh, 2000). *Traffic* was a huge earner for the company with a US box office gross of $124,107,477 on a budget of $51 million that Soderbergh reputably and famously delivered for $49 million.[12] USA Films was also the distributor of *Being John Malkovich* (Jonze, 1999), and both co-producer and distributor of *Gosford Park* (Altman, 2001). Like Good Machine, USA Films also forged important links with queer filmmakers, Gus Van Sant in particular, as deals made in 2000 between USA Films and Van Sant's Meno Films became springboards for the production and release of *Elephant* (2003) and *Paranoid Park* (2007). The success of these collaborations became instrumental in the more recent high profile partnership between Van Sant and Focus Features on *Milk*.[13]

USA Films was originally formed by media entrepreneur Barry Diller in 1999 after the merger of two independent film distributors: Gramercy Pictures (then co-owned by Polygram and Universal) and October Films (independent until it was acquired by Universal in 1997). USA Films was in effect a renaming of October Films and would soon see itself merge with Universal's subsidiaries Studio Canal and Universal Focus. Scott Greenstein, previously a senior vice president with Miramax, was the first executive appointed at USA Films, but was subsequently fired and the reins of the company were entrusted to Schamus. Schamus was already connected to USA Films in one capacity as Good Machine was the company that handled the international distribution of USA Films.

In 2000 USA Films divided $100 million film finance between fifteen productions, of which seven were in-house (including a few made for television and DVD premieres such as *Firestarter 2: Rekindled* [Iscove, 2002]) and four were acquisitions of independent productions (including Neil La Bute's *Nurse Betty* [2000], which was a Gramercy production), while the remainder of the finance was spent on co-financing productions in partnership with other independent companies. According to *Variety*, USA Films' business practices were unusual for a company of its size, feeding further questions about the company's position in the industry, especially in terms of whether it was independent or studio in orientation. *Variety's* speculation about USA Films' future as uncertain (especially as at the time of the article in question there were no new USA productions slated) can be read retrospectively as symptomatic of the significant changes behind the scenes that would see Focus Features loom on the horizon. What seemed to be *Variety's* bugbear was that USA Films' industry position was relatively unclear, a position situated between the independent and studio worlds and characterised by USA Films' 'arrangement with Universal wherein the speciality label has the opportunity to make or distribute projects more suitable to its needs'.[14] It is this lack of discernable separation suggested by such 'arrangements' that contributes to the problems of definition of independent cinema and to the need for a re-definition that the term 'indie' implies.

Focus Features

'One thing that defines Focus is we make movies that are not for everybody.'[15]

Focus Features was created in 2002 out of the consolidation of three of Universal's specialty divisions (USA Films, Studio Canal US,[16] and Universal Focus[17]) and the acquisition of James Schamus and Ted Hope's Good Machine. Therefore, and unlike the other specialty divisions, Focus Features was created from both a merging of existing subsidiaries and the acquisition of an independent company. As early as January 2000, *Variety* was already reporting on moves within Universal to create an autonomous subsidiary division that could eventually compete with Miramax for dominance in the lucrative specialty market.[18] Focus Features eventually took shape with James Schamus and David Linde as co-heads of Universal's new speciality division. Despite prior speculation that the chief executive officer post was going to be filled by Scott Greenstein, the end result was a smart combination of Good Machine's Schamus and USA Films' Linde as both those companies had an established pedigree and expertise, which was immediately brought in to Focus: Good Machine's track record in foreign sales operations complemented well USA Films' healthy production slate.

In the first few years of operation the initial strength of Focus Features was the general and steady growth of the company which was certainly helped by the critical and commercial success of a number of high profile European acquisitions, including *The Pianist* (Roman Polanski, 2002) and *Swimming Pool* (François Ozon, 2003) in addition to its two co-produced indie favourites *Far From Heaven* (Haynes, 2002) and *Lost in Translation* (Sofia Coppola, 2003) – the last two also subjects of volumes in the American Indies series. From its initial roster of acquisitions and productions, Focus Features demonstrated a strong investment in authorship and left-field productions that has distinguished the company as a quality brand with prestige and kudos. This can also be seen in the company's mission statement which presents Focus Features as a 'company committed to bringing moviegoers the most original stories from the world's most innovative filmmakers'.[19] The emphasis on originality and innovation is clearly imbedded in the discourse of authorship that has been a driving force in the romanticised vision of contemporary American independent cinema. This recent incarnation of American independent cinema commenced in the late 1970s with strong authorial figures like John Sayles, Jim Jarmusch and Wayne Wang as well as a small number of independent distributors, such as First Run Features, and early studio classics divisions such as United Artists Classics, who specialised in the distribution of the auteur-driven European Art Cinema.

Central to Focus Features as a brand is the significant number of Academy, Independent Spirit and Golden Globe Awards in addition to countless critical and festival awards for films that the company has either distributed, produced, or both. Focus Features first made its splash in the film world with *The Pianist*, a film that it distributed in the North American market and subsequently garnered three Academy Awards, alongside *Far From Heaven* which was nominated for four Oscars and Golden Globes and which won three Independent Spirit Awards for best director, best film, and best female lead. This remarkable immediate success was quickly followed in 2003 by *Lost in Translation*'s Oscar win for Best Original Screenplay and nominations for Best Picture, Actor and Director, and its sweep of the Independent Spirit Awards.

In subsequent years, notable Focus Features successes include its high-profile Oscar presence with *Eternal Sunshine of the Spotless Mind* (Gondry, 2004), its two European acquisitions *The Constant Gardner* (Meirelles, 2005) and *Atonement* (Joe Wright, 2007), and more recently *Milk* (six nominations and two wins for Best Actor and Best Original Screenplay at the 2008 Academy Awards).

Brokeback Mountain was a major awards success story for Focus Features in 2006. Although the film controversially lost the Award for Best Picture to *Crash* (Paul Haggis, 2004) it still managed to win awards for Best Director, Best Score and Best Adapted Screenplay to add to its Golden Globe wins for best director and best film and its awards for best director and best film at the 2005 Independent Spirit Awards. These results certainly suggest that Focus has had a remarkable expertise in cultivating and predicting award success both in its acquisitions and its productions, which often translate to financial remuneration. Equally importantly, such a success demonstrates clearly that the company has started occupying the space that was reserved for Miramax in the 1990s, especially as the latter gradually moved to blockbuster productions such as *Gangs of New York* (Scorsese, 2002) and *The Aviator* (Scorsese, 2004).

In 2006 David Linde left his position as co-chair of Focus Features for an executive position at the parent company, Universal. The same year marked a downturn for Focus as despite the success of *Brokeback Mountain* and its Oscar glory, the company was only involved in one production that year, *Hollywoodland* (Coulter, 2006). Following Linde's departure, assumptions about the uncertainty of Focus Features started circulating, often based on the stereotypical view that the company had always been divided between on the one hand, David Linde's head for business and panache in deal-making and, on the other, the creativity and taste-making that apparently characterised James Schamus. Linde's ascension in the Universal ranks was followed in 2007 by Focus Features' emphasis on productions rather than acquisitions with only five titles slated as Focus Features films and two genre films under the banner of the recently formed sister company Rogue Pictures.[20] 2007 also saw a new venture with one of the largest book publishers in the world, Random House, to create Random House Pictures. The new company was conceived as an organisation that would streamline operations with regard to film adaptations of particular titles from the numerous Random House imprints but, until the time of writing (September 2009), no such film releases had materialised.

It would appear from Focus Features' current production and distribution slate (in 2008 and 2009 the company upped its release slate to eight and thirteen films respectively, following the critical and commercial success of *Burn after Reading* [Joel Coen, 2008] and *Milk*) that the company has been a successful entity, with around ninety films chalked up between distribution and production since 2002. In an industry that is rife with unpredictability, subsidiary closures, a constantly changing executive personnel and, currently, a global financial crisis, Focus Features seems to have earned its place in the American film industry. Still led by James Schamus and with its brand of quality still being a major attraction for auteur-driven filmmakers, Focus Features' short-term future at least seems to be secure. Despite a disastrous year for a number of specialty labels (such as Paramount Vantage, Picturehouse, Warner Independent Pictures and Miramax, which were subsumed in their parent company, Vantage, folded [Picturehouse and WIP] and downsized [Miramax]), Focus Features has announced significant indie releases by well-known filmmakers such as Ang Lee (*Taking Woodstock*), Jim Jarmusch (*The Limits of Control*) and Sofia Coppola (*Somewhere*). Table 2 contains all Focus Features productions between 2002 and 2009.

Indies as Classics Divisions

Along with Focus Features, the current slate of the majors' classics divisions include Fox Searchlight (1994–), Sony Pictures Classics (1992–), Paramount Vantage (formerly Paramount Classics; 1998–), United Artists Films (1999–) and Miramax (1989–). The majority of these studio subsidiaries were formed in the mid-/late-1990s and have been characterised as the indie cinema's 'microcosm of the studio business'.[21] One should also add to this list Lionsgate, the only truly independent outfit with multiplex presence that has no ties with a parent company or a larger conglomerate for its finance and distribution.[22] However, despite some similarities with the classics divisions, Lionsgate's predilection for cheap genre films, especially horror, has rarely enabled the company to be perceived at the same level as those studio specialty labels which are mostly in the business of quality, auteur-driven films.

The idea of an independent cinema that mirrors Hollywood, especially in terms of business practices, has been severely criticised by spokespeople for smaller production outfits that do not benefit from ties with studios. Christine Vachon, the independent producer and

Table 2 Focus Features productions 2002–8

Film	Year	Director
Possession	2002	Neil LaBute
Far From Heaven	2002	Todd Haynes
They	2002	Robert Harmon
How to Deal	2003	Claire Kilner
Lost in Translation	2003	Sofia Coppola
The Texas Chainsaw Massacre	2003	Marcus Nispel
Sylvia	2003	Christine Jeffs
Eternal Sunshine of the Spotless Mind	2004	Michel Gondry
The Door in the Floor	2004	Tod Williams
Vanity Fair	2004	Mira Nair
Assault on Precinct 13	2005	Jean François Richet
Broken Flowers	2005	Jim Jarmusch
Brokeback Mountain	2005	Ang Lee
Imagine Me and You	2005	Ol Parker
Block Party	2005	Michel Gondry
Prime	2005	Ben Younger
Hollywoodland	2006	Allen Coulter
The Hitcher	2007	Dave Meyers
Lust, Caution	2007	Ang Lee
Eastern Promises	2007	David Cronenberg
Reservation Road	2007	Terry George
Dan in Real Life	2007	Peter Hedges
In Bruges	2008	Martin McDonagh
Be Kind Rewind	2008	Michel Gondry
The Other Boleyn Girl	2008	Justin Chadwick
Milk	2008	Gus Van Sant
Rudo y Cursi	2008	Carlos Cuarón
True Legend	2009	Yuen Woo-Ping
Biutiful	2009	Alejandro González Iñárritu
Thirst	2009	Park Chan-wook
Taking Woodstock	2009	Ang Lee
Murderer	2009	Yeung Chow Hin Roy
9	2009	Shane Acker
The Warrior and the Wolf	2009	Tian Zhuangzhuang

president of Killer Films, voiced great concern when she explained the current situation for independent films in the following way:

Not only is the line between studio and independent films completely blurred from a financing standpoint, but audiences have lost a certain appetite for filmmaking that is essentially experimental in nature, so that even independent films look, sound, and feel (in form and content) like commercial studio films.[23]

When Focus Features was first established, one of its initial mandates was to distribute non-US films in the North American (USA and Canada) market. As a matter of fact, a central aspect of all classics divisions' operations has traditionally been to continue to fulfil this acquisition and distribution role for their respective parent companies, as long as the market for foreign films in North America continued to be buoyant. However, in recent years this mandate has been severely tested as the classics divisions gradually shifted from their acquisition and distribution role towards one that is primarily characterised by the finance and production of in-house films. This shift, it could be argued, is mirrored in the move from an American independent film (as separate from Hollywood and the media conglomerates) to indie film with its blatant ties to the major studios. Although smaller companies also try to participate in this newly perceived indie cinema, most of the successful recent indie film productions are products of the studios' specialty arms, as their respective parent companies have empowered them with financial backing that is simply not available to small independents.

Furthermore, the existence of the classics division frees up the parent companies, which can now focus solely on their big event films, franchise-driven blockbuster films and star vehicles. In this respect, Universal as a Hollywood brand can take a step back, both institutionally and ideologically, from direct investment and promotion of its subsidiary's films, such as *Brokeback Mountain*. As Focus Features was involved in making *Brokeback Mountain* a commercial hit through its knowledge of and expertise in the specialty film market, parent company Universal was able to concentrate on the huge benefits of distributing *King Kong* (Peter Jackson, 2005) and *The Producers* (Stroman, 2005), both extremely well-established titles.

One could argue then that classics divisions are able to 'independently' focus on the production of smaller and mid-budget pictures that the studios no longer directly deal with (and do not have the acumen to do so). This is especially the case with films that are risky financial gambles and are characterised by 'edgier' content (paradoxically the bestiality and rampant racism of Universal's *King Kong* is not considered as problematic as two cowboys in love). It could also be argued that the indie films of the classics divisions exist in an in-between position of two industrial and institutional contexts, straddling the two polarities, formerly autonomous yet positioned somewhere in the role of producing and distributing low key and mid-budget pictures that their parents no longer seem committed to producing.

American Indies, a cinema driven by the classics divisions, has both benefited from the industrial location of its producing agencies and succumbed to varying degrees of interference from these agencies' corporate parents. There is no uniform story as to how an independent film fares under a studio-backed production regime and it is arguably too early for succinct historical periodisation; there are both good and bad stories. The benefits to independent cinema through the classics divisions are open to debate and speculation. Independent films are being invested in and heavily promoted, distributed and exhibited to a wider audience than ever before, allowing audiences to appreciate and develop a taste for indie films of popular acclaim such as *Little Miss Sunshine* (Dayton and Faris, 2006). On the other hand, these films might be seen to be also compromised right from the beginning. Are they less experimental in style than they used to be before the recent changes in the classics divisions? Are they less ideologically challenging than the independent films of the 1980s? Does this actually matter?

All these questions beg an arguably more important question within the context of this book: are the truly independent features those films that do not have any studio ties and have struggled consistently for production funds, distribution deals, marketing budgets, etc., before eventually being pushed to a marginal position and seen by very few people? Or is an indie film like *Brokeback Mountain* more important as it does afford ample visibility and exposure to the gay community? Although it is too soon to provide a comprehensive answer to this question, the first signs are certainly not promising as the visibility of queer, gay and lesbian films immediately following *Brokeback Mountain*, with the arguable exception of *Milk*, remained the same as before the film appeared: that is, nowhere to be found in the venues currently inhabited by what we are now calling indie films.

In order to provide a more complete mapping of the current situation, that is, indies as beneficiaries of studio-led arrangements, this chapter will now move into outlining six key areas of operation and definition that characterise Focus Features and the larger contemporary indie film landscape.

1. Financial Backing

Films produced and distributed under Focus Features are financially backed by Universal, which allocates a budget for its subsidiary to finance films up to a certain limit. For example, in 2004 Focus could finance films with a budget of up to $30 million.[24] This necessarily suggests that studio and media conglomerate power is shaping indie cinema through their high level decisions regarding fund allocations and explains why increasingly higher budget ceilings are introduced for indie films. In this respect, it is clear that the decision about what an average indie film costs is determined higher up the chain than the classics division itself, which makes the financing, production and distribution of 'truly' independent films problematic.

2. Cut-price Rates for Talent

Focus Features also benefits from its status as independent in that it does not necessarily offer stars studio rates and similar financial arrangements. The company can secure stars such as Bill Murray (in *Lost in Translation* and *Broken Flowers* [Jarmusch, 2005]), Sean Penn (in *Milk*) and Julianne Moore (in *Far From Heaven*) for rates well below their normal asking price for a studio picture. It is also understood that stars want to work in the independent sector for their own cultural capital, allowing their talent to be framed in relation to creativity rather than commerce. Jake Gyllenhaal is a good example of an actor who frequently moves between independent and studio production, going from *The Day After Tomorrow* (Emmerich, 2004) to *Brokeback Mountain*. However, there is also a flipside with many stars who forged an early career in independent cinema deciding to sever their ties with the independent sector after establishing themselves in studio pictures. For instance, Heather Matarazzo was distinguished as a geeky teenager in Todd Solondz's *Welcome to the Dollhouse* (1995), but after appearing in Disney's *The Princess Diaries* (Gary Marshall, 2001) no longer wished to be associated with Solondz's work.[25]

Independent film can often be a stepping-stone rather than an ongoing alternative to studio work, especially if the work is in low-budget genre fare. Furthermore, it is not always the case that stars will work for reduced rates as USA Films' budget for *Traffic* jumped $10 million to pay for Michael Douglas's fee.[26] One such salary 'scandal' surrounded *Brokeback Mountain* too. Randy Quaid who played the supporting character of Joe Aguirre, the man who employs Ennis and Jack to tend the sheep, sued Focus Features for $10 million in damages for deferred payment because Quaid was working under the assumption that *Brokeback Mountain* would be a low-key independent film and not the commercial success it turned out to be.[27] Quaid claimed that Focus Features exploited him as if the indie outfit was laundering money knowing full well that the film would be a hit. Quaid's lawsuit was withdrawn and never made it to court; however, this small debacle draws attention to potential grievances between actors, salaries and the financial arrangements in the indie context. Indie films do set their sights on economic success as well as artistic credibility and both actors and stars are central to this.

3. Marketing

Overall the classics divisions have brought a mainstream presence to independent film through a greater emphasis on marketing and publicity. Indie films are characterised by strongly defined marketing images that get disseminated with maximum exposure. Key images from indie films are also limited to one or two main graphic designs. In *Brokeback Mountain*'s case there was only one design in circulation, a close-up of Gyllenhaal and Ledger in close proximity but each moving in a different direction. Studio backing has resulted in an increase in the visibility of independent films on a scale hitherto unprecedented because the money is now available to the subsidiaries to saturate markets with posters, press releases, film trailers, television spots, making of documentaries, etc. As Justin Wyatt once noted in reference to Miramax, the centrality of marketing, especially the repackaging of films through the foregrounding of aspects that often are not central to the films, was part of the independent company's phenomenal success during this period.[28]

Former Miramax marketing executive David Brooks joined Focus Features as president of marketing in 2002.[29] The strong marketing presence that Brooks's tenure at Miramax brought to Focus translated into the instantly identifiable posters of the films *Lost in Translation*, *Far From Heaven* and *Brokeback Mountain*, which appeared on bus shelters, in magazines, on television and in many other prominent places. In Ang Lee's native Taiwan, *Brokeback Mountain* was even promoted through the Starbucks coffee chain, which positioned the film within a wider web of global consumerism. At the time of the DVD release of *Juno*, the indie film *par excellence*, the film was being advertised on every available space in a local shopping mall in Nottingham including elevator doors and, ironically, rubbish bins in what can only be interpreted as a gesture at the film's imagined obsolescence. For a time it was nearly impossible to avoid multiple confrontations with *Juno* within the space of a few minutes.

This clearly suggests that while independent films were once those films that one had to seek out at in art cinemas and repertory playhouses, in recent years one can find indie films like *Broken Flowers* playing at both the art house and the multiplex simultaneously. Indies are really hard to miss these days and this is a result of intense marketing and promotion strategies, all of which require the extent of financial backing once reserved for studio picture promotion. Furthermore, indies are being heavily advertised in places which seem ideologically remote from the assumptions one would make about independent cinema's politics. David Linde highlighted the marketing drive of indie cinema when he proposed a high concept model for independent cinema;[30] once the reserve of studios, high concept is now becoming a standard practice in the indie sector.

4. Crossover Potential and Mainstream Success

With such powerful studio-backed marketing machines driving the indie sector, the clear objective for the films produced and distributed is to cross over. Once a pleasant surprise and a rare occurrence, crossing over has gradually become an expectation for indie films. A film that crosses over is one that shifts from a marginal position, known by a select few, to a mainstream position, known by a filmgoing majority. This can also be the effect of the film's distribution pattern, released in a few key cities to generate buzz before going on a nationwide release. In the 2000s Focus Features has become a name that has been heavily associated with a number of quirky must-see key indie crossovers, such as *Lost in Translation*, *Far from Heaven*, *Eternal Sunshine of the Spotless Mind*, *Brokeback Mountain* and *Milk*, films that have found a place in popular film culture after generating a buzz that is usually reserved for much more commercially present and heavily promoted event pictures, big budget genre vehicles and star-driven features.

5. Ancillary Markets and Release Patterns

The classics divisions also benefit from their parent companies' greater access to ancillary markets, especially through cable television and domestic DVD sales arrangements. For example, in 2003 Universal had pay deals with premium US cable channels HBO and Starz Encore for a number of its films.[31] This arrangement extended to its subsidiary's films, which meant that indie features could also benefit from the same vast ancillary markets that until recently have been open only for studio pictures. Universal and the other majors also rely on their indie subsidiaries to generate content that will help beef up the package of titles for DVD sales and provide enough films for a cable and network television deal. DVD releases of indie films quickly become available in the sell-through market after theatrical exhibition and no longer have lengthy theatrical runs in a limited number of prints on a select few screens.

In 2005 Focus had deals in place with Virgin Megastores and other media outlets to target consumers with special Focus Features DVD stands that would show off the company as a quality brand.[32] *Brokeback Mountain*'s US theatrical release in December 2005 (January 2006 everywhere else) was soon followed by a US DVD release in March 2006, only three months after its release date in the major US cities. Following a short period at full cost in the domestic sell-through market (approximately three months), the *Brokeback Mountain* DVD was very quickly discounted and on special offer at low prices, often tied to 'buy one get one free' deals alongside other Universal DVD releases in every major high street media chain and supermarket. Less than a year later, in January 2007, *Brokeback Mountain* was re-released on DVD in the USA as a double disc special edition with virtually no extra content. Other indie films tend to follow a similar release, distribution and sale pattern for a speedy turnaround from theatrical exhibition to domestic purchase and then premium cable broadcast within 12 months. In this respect, the indie film's new-found access to the highly profitable ancillary markets has led to new revenue channels and increased exposure. This is especially important as potential losses in the theatrical market are often recouped through success in the ancillary markets.

6. Sister Companies and Genre Franchises

The contemporary indie sector is further divided into its own subsubsidiaries or sister companies as a clear sign of its growing commercial interests. This is further evidence of the importance of the ancillary markets and the role of mid-budget studio film production taking root in the classics division. In turn, this also expands the definition of indie cinema which now also includes straight-up genre pictures. This is a move to expand into more lucrative territory through genre films targeted to specific audience demographics, especially films which have the potential to generate low-cost quick-return franchises. One could indeed argue that identifying and exploiting franchise potential seems to be wholly characteristic of the sub-subsidiaries. This situation also recalls the production of the slasher movie franchises from the early 1980s, like *Friday the 13th* (Cunningham, 1980) and *A Nightmare on Elm Street* (Craven, 1984). These films were made for a very low cost by independent companies but generated very high returns through extensive studio marketing and distribution (Paramount in the case of *Friday the 13th*). The contemporary model for this move to genre production is Dimension Films, formerly a subsidiary of Miramax and currently residing with the Weinstein Company after the departure of Bob and Harvey Weinstein from Miramax, Disney and Buena Vista.

Dimension Films, like Miramax, is both a producer and a distributor and made inroads in the 1990s within the horror franchise market as well as the release of dubbed, edited, and hip-hopified Hong Kong martial arts films starring Jet Li. Alisa Perren has suggested that despite the talent moving across subsidiary and sister, the company executives of Miramax and Dimension also sought to reinforce brand divisions in order to produce different identities for each of the speciality monikers in ways that culturally value one over the other.[33] Focus Features followed this pattern, establishing in March 2004 its own subsidiary sister brand called Rogue Pictures.[34] The name Rogue Pictures was already in circulation a few years prior to this deal but shuffling the sister company in with Schamus and Linde through Focus Features was an attempt to mirror the relationship between Miramax and Dimension. Under Focus Features, Rogue's emphasis, according to *Variety*, was initially geared towards in-house productions rather than acquisitions. However, an examination of the company's output suggests that the company concentrated on distribution, releasing twenty-five titles in the period between 2004 and 2009.[35]

In January 2009, Universal sold Rogue Pictures and its library for $150m to Relativity Media but maintained the right to still distribute Rogue Pictures theatrically at a discounted distribution rate.[36] Rogue Pictures operated to produce and distribute genre features both for theatrical exhibition and for the DVD premieres market. DVD premieres, formerly known as 'straight-to-video', are feature films produced solely for a domestic DVD release and subsequently for premiere cable broadcast. Rogue Pictures' first releases were the production and distribution

Table 3 Rogue Pictures productions, US distributions, DVD premiers 2004–8

Title	Year	Director	Company role
Seed of Chucky	2004	Don Mancini	Producer/distributor
Shaun of the Dead	2004	Edgar Wright	Distributor
Assault on Precinct 13	2005	Jean François Richet	Producer/distributor
Carlito's Way: Rise to Power	2005	Michael Bregman	Producer/DVD premiere
Danny the Dog	2005	Louis Leterier	Distributor
Cry_Wolf	2005	Jeff Wadlow	Distributor
Block Party*	2005	Michel Gondry	Distributor
American Pie: Band Camp	2005	Steve Rash	Producer/DVD premiere
Waist Deep	2005	Vondie Cutis-Hall	Producer/distributor
The Return	2006	Asif Kapadia	Producer/distributor
Fearless	2006	Ronny Yu	Distributor
American Pie: Naked Mile	2006	Joe Nussbaum	Producer/distributor
Altered	2006	Eduardo Sánchez	Distributor
The Hitcher*	2007	Dave Meyers	Distributor
Balls of Fury	2007	Robert Ben Garant	Producer/distributor
Hot Fuzz	2007	Edgar Wright	Distributor
White Noise 2: The Light	2007	Patrick Lussier	Distributor
American Pie: Beta House	2007	Andrew Waller	Producer/DVD premiere
Doomsday	2008	Neil Marshall	Producer/distributor
The Strangers	2008	Bryan Bertino	Producer/distributor

*   Focus Features production

of *Seed Of Chucky* (Mancini, 2004), an entry in the *Child's Play* horror franchise, and the remake of John Carpenter's cult classic *Assault on Precinct 13* (Richet, 2005). Rogue Pictures was the US distributor of the British horror comedy *Shaun of the Dead* (Edgar Wright, 2004), and financed the straight-to-DVD release *Carlito's Way: Rise To Power* (Michael Bregman, 2005) in addition to a number of straight-to-video sequels in the teen comedy franchise *American Pie*. Table 3 provides a comprehensive list of Rogue Pictures' films.

Conclusion: Indies as a Force of Nature?

The driving force behind this transformation in the independent cinema sector and its shift to indie cinema has been an unprecedented commercialisation that was brought on by the dominance of a new organisational structure. When specialty divisions shifted from their original role of film acquisition and distribution companies into producers and distributors of independent films, they changed the very meaning of independence. While this commercialisation has brought indie films to a much wider audience, it has also had negative consequences for films with no commercial design, whether stylistically or ideologically, which are finding it increasingly hard to get even modest distribution. These consequences can be seen on independently produced queer, gay and lesbian films which are often not properly assimilated into the indie realm; *Juno*'s abortion angst is almost cute and acceptable but gay romance, let alone gay sex, is still iffy. Those queer films that do find a classics division for distribution through pre-sales are often recounted as very troubled productions replete with interference. Two such examples are *Boys Don't Cry* (Kimberley Pierce, 1999) and *A Home at The End of the World* (Michael Mayer, 2005), with the latter reported to have gone through 'big-picture studio scrutiny' for an 'off-beat little picture'.[37]

The problems that those two films faced make *Brokeback Mountain* all the more unusual as the one film with explicitly queer content that was not constrained by the problems and interference meted out to other similarly themed films. However, despite its critical and commercial success, *Brokeback Mountain* did not generate a new wave of queer indies with crossover potential, as was often speculated during the film's peak. *Brokeback Mountain* did not make American cinema, or even indie cinema, less resistant to queer material. It has also had its fair share of criticism from both the right and the left as well as by dissenting voices from the gay press, and frustration by 'truly' independent gay filmmakers and producers. Yet *Brokeback Mountain* still stands as a testament to the potential and the possibilities that the indie sector offers, however commercially driven, to sometimes get it right. Despite the concerned suggestions in this chapter at the underlying logic of indie cinema's commercial drive and its effects on independent cinema more generally, the classics divisions can still produce and distribute films which defy expectations, as I believe *Brokeback Mountain* does.

This chapter has sought to define the new terrain of independent cinema as one that is more constructive to be labelled indie cinema. As a type of cinema positioned in relation to studio parents and conglomerate empires, indie cinema bridges the studios and the independents, once radically opposed to one another through production practices and politics, and brings to the screen 'glossy award hopefuls and edgier fare'.[38] *Brokeback Mountain* occupies the space between independent film and studio picture, glossy yet edgy and with film stars who are yet convincing in scenes of gay intimacy. In many ways *Brokeback Mountain* is resistant to the 'either/or' approach of independent and studio definitions as the film is both radical and conventional at the same time and solicits the interpretational impasse that Eve Kosofsky Sedgwick calls 'kinda subversive, kinda hegemonic'.[39] *Brokeback Mountain*'s queerness challenges us to think about, or even possibly question, the usefulness of boundaries and categories, not just between the film's genre leanings as both melodrama and Western, or between straight and gay masculinities, but also the troubled distinction between the old independent and the new indie.

2. Queering the Western

Introduction: Is *Brokeback Mountain* a Western?

Is *Brokeback Mountain* a Western? This could be a divisive question that implicates the viewer in accepting or rejecting that a much-cherished genre has a queer history. If *Brokeback Mountain* is a Western this implies that homosexual desires and gay men, to whatever degree sublimated, have always been part of the narrative and logic of this Hollywood genre. By extension, one would also need to accommodate a queer history within a larger mythological and epic story of fashioning the American West. The answer to this key question is one that also makes difficult a separation from the processes of reception as our identity is often brought to bear on how we make genre meaningful. One thing is clear, which is that homophobic responses to *Brokeback Mountain* often resist viewing the film as a Western, opting instead to see it as completely antithetical to, more often than not a perverted mockery of, the Western. Such a reading perceives *Brokeback Mountain* as a straight-up attack on 'American values', a perverse film neatly summed up in the title of one widely-read virulent response subtitled 'Rape of the Marlboro Man'.[1]

Such homophobia is quite revealing because it is precisely the way in which *Brokeback Mountain* appears to be a Western with 'regular guys' that in effect produces the homophobic response in the first place. Had it not impinged on the sanctity of the Western, contaminating it with homo desires, perhaps *Brokeback Mountain* would have generated much less homophobia and certainly less cultural parody. The latter I consider to be a strategy of containment – aren't gay cowboys just silly – a plain refusal to accommodate same-sex desires in Western mythology. In response to the opening question of this chapter, a queer retort might intervene and ask, if the Western is so 'straight' then why the need to defend it?

This chapter has two aims and due to its length it is organised in two main sections. The first section has the rather obvious aim of examining *Brokeback Mountain* in relation to film scholarship on the Western. Specifically, I will explore *Brokeback Mountain*'s generic conformity and deviation from some of the texts that initially made the Western in particular, and film genre in general, such rich objects of study. Furthermore, I am interested in how *Brokeback Mountain* prompts one to productively introduce queer theory to the Western genre. This discussion will lead to the second section of the chapter in which my aim is to open up *Brokeback Mountain*'s connection to a longer history of relations between the Western genre and homosexuality. This requires me to operate at a tangent from *Brokeback Mountain* by discussing several other films. It is my aim to claim *Brokeback Mountain* for a context that views the film not only within the history of the Western, but also within an equally enduring history of homosexual and queer relationships with the genre. While the focus of the chapter is *Brokeback Mountain* it is difficult to avoid detours as the film functions heuristically, that is, it provides the impetus to examine several other instances where the Western and homosexuality bristle against one another in a seductive and illuminating way. The intent here is not to provide an overarching queer history of the Western (that would be a book length study in itself). Rather, I would like to explore various nodal points of interest that gesture towards an alternative history of the Western in which *Brokeback Mountain* is only the latest instalment. B. Ruby Rich, one of the first queer critics to view the film, and the critic who coined the term New Queer Cinema, anticipated the significance of *Brokeback Mountain* as a soon to explode film that would be understood as a queer Western.[2] A few months before the film's general release, Ruby Rich was already suggesting that *Brokeback Mountain* goes beyond previous Westerns, turning 'text and subtext inside out' viewing 'the history of the West back through an uncompromisingly queer lens'.[3] Ruby Rich's remarks in many ways provide the stimulus to explore in more detail *Brokeback Mountain*'s queering of the Western and its place within a more enduring and queerer history of the genre.

A Gay Cowboy Movie?

While in production with Focus Features, and even after its release in 2005, *Brokeback Mountain* was often referred to as 'the gay cowboy movie' or 'a cowboy romance'.[4] A considerable amount of speculation, expectation and disapproval attached to the film was generated in the associations between the terms 'gay' and 'cowboy' appearing in the same sentence and in the way *Brokeback Mountain*, perhaps knowingly, gestured towards a well-kept secret: that American mythology, homosexuality and a Hollywood film genre have been mutual bedfellows on more than one occasion. Ang Lee repeatedly dissuaded the reading of the film as a Western in favour of the more universalised and depoliticised adoption of humanism. *Brokeback Mountain* was the tragic romance par excellence, with Lee calling the film 'a great American love story' when receiving the Golden Lion for Best Film at the Venice Film Festival. Lee even went as far as to make a profoundly un-queer analogy when he told *The Independent* newspaper that 'it's a great romantic tragedy like *Romeo and Juliet*'.[5]

Not content with pointing out the film's lineage in hetero-tragedy, the film's genre was also, and rather problematically, attached to the 'universal love story' moniker and according to Jack Foley, president of distribution at Focus Features, *Brokeback Mountain* was also 'a very human story'.[6] As a matter of fact, *Brokeback Mountain* was not only linked to the *Romeo and Juliet* plot but was even touted as the new *Titanic* (obviously in weeping quota rather than revenue). Such a vague and general though frequently drawn set of relations clearly works to de-gay *Brokeback Mountain* from being a film about homophobia and the closet. It also goes against the account of Jack and Ennis's existence by Annie Proulx, who described her novella as a 'story of destructive rural homophobia'.[7] And it fails to take into consideration the temporally and spatially specific milieu in which the story takes place. The institutional spin coming from the production sought to align *Brokeback Mountain* with any genre other than the Western and in turn help deflect those themes imagined to be alien to the genre. Whether intentional or not, this strategy was designed with a view to broadening the film's appeal by stressing familiarity, universality and the theme of the great American tragedy, rather than Proulx's 'destructive rural homophobia'.

At the same time, there was a persistent trend in the critical and journalistic terrain of reading *Brokeback Mountain*, rather superficially it should be said, precisely through the very genre that the film was apparently not an example of. Among other things, this conflict of definition clearly demonstrates how genre is made meaningful in ways that are often beyond the text and its institutional and authorial intent. Ang Lee's disavowals would remain unheeded as critics and reviewers of the film would only see *Brokeback Mountain* as a Western or a cowboy movie. In claiming *Brokeback Mountain* for the Western, a good deal of the popular and lay assessment of the film tended to renege any actual insight into the film as an example of the Western genre, opting instead to use *Brokeback Mountain* as a case study for a joking and light-hearted reassessment of the Western as a genre that had produced films in which characters demonstrate latent and manifest homosexual tendencies.

However, accepting *Brokeback Mountain* as simply a 'gay Western' or 'gay cowboy movie', even in the vaguest sense of what that might mean, is to also place homosexuality and even queerness in the narrative of American mythology. To deny *Brokeback Mountain*'s place within the Western genre is also to discount the ways in which the film reworks the Western formula through a specific set of political concerns that relates a troubled history of homosexuality and desire through national mythology and popular genre. A general tendency of film scholars of the Western is to highlight the genre's role in making sense of national and cultural identity; it is clear that viewing *Brokeback Mountain* as a queer Western becomes an important strategy in writing homosexuality in to that history. The mythological narrative has regulated out of its story any notion of homosexuality in the West even as such myths are charac-terised by an overinvestment in all-male kinship. Chris Packard's *Queer Cowboys* is a recent historical corrective that assesses the all-male culture of the American West.[8] Packard's focus is actually on the literature of the period but his observations apply equally to the place occupied by the film genre when he suggests the following:

If there is something national about the cowboy (and the frontier heroes of his ilk), and if there is something homoerotic about the partnerships he forms in the wilderness, then there is something homoerotic about American national identity as the literary West conceives it.[9]

In his influential study of film genres, Thomas Schatz suggested that as a Hollywood genre 'the Western represents American culture, explaining its present in terms of its past and virtually redefining the past to accommodate the present',[10] a point that Ed Buscombe and Roberta Pearson reiterated in *Back in the Saddle Again* when they suggested that the Western's 'various cultural forms also attest to the central role it contin-ues to play in conceptions of national identity'.[11] Given the centrality of the genre in American national and cultural politics, it would seem to be far from coincidental that *Brokeback Mountain* appeared at a time when the hegemony of heterosexual marriage in the USA was being challenged by the demands of same-sex partnership rights.[12] Indeed, the film explodes the hitherto repressed relations between multiple male same-sex configurations and their place in national mythmaking. While this is a timely coup for indexing sexuality in relation to the national, political and cultural issues it is not entirely a cause for celebration, since what still persists in the Western's many discourses, if they are understood to be couched in a wider context of national and cultural myth, is the ongoing erasure of women and lesbians. *Brokeback Mountain* is typical as a Western in that it continues to be a genre whose interest is centred on men, one quite literally obsessed with man-on-man action.

In an article on *Brokeback Mountain* Jim Kitses calls the Western an 'unfashionably ancient genre'.[13] Yet, the Western is one of the oldest American film genres and seems to be a fairly resilient and persistent form. Ever so sporadically Westerns appear on our cinema screens accompanied by the same claims that on the one hand, the Western is a long dead Hollywood relic and on the other, the Western is coming back in fashion. Many of the contemporary (post-1960s) Westerns extend the definition of the genre and tend to work self-consciously using the spectator's familiarity with and knowledge of the generic conventions in order to provide interesting reworkings of the formula as well as examine contemporaneous political ideas or ideological debates. These tend to take various forms and shapes, including the reassessment of historical events, the questioning of masculinity, or the more accurate re-inscription of the complexities of race, ethnicity and gender during the 'epic moment'. Westerns are still made because the genre can still usefully tell us something about cultural politics. Sometimes though, as is the case with the remake of *3:10 to Yuma* (Mangold, 2007), Westerns would occasionally seem to be produced for the simple generic pleasures they still provide.

The buzzword for what the Western is often claimed to accomplish as a contemporary version of an ageing genre is 'revisionism'. The modern or neo-Westerns that are often claimed in the name of revisionism are, among others, *Little Big Man* (Penn, 1970) *Buffalo Bill and the Indians, or Sitting Bull's History Lesson* (Altman, 1976), *Dances with Wolves* (Costner, 1990) and *Unforgiven* (Eastwood, 1992). The revisionist impulse also implies that the spectator would be more intellectually engaged, fully aware of the ideologically transparent role that the Western plays, especially when it comes to identity politics. Revisionist Westerns are generally post-1960s, produced and released at a time when independent filmmaking had started to manifest itself as a viable alternative to Hollywood cinema. In this respect, it comes as no surprise that the most significant revisions of the past twenty years have come from the more aesthetically and ideologically challenging independent film sector. A far from exhaustive list of more recent independent Westerns would include *Lust in the Dust* (Bartel, 1985), *Smoke Signals* (Eyre, 1988), *Lone Star* (Sayles, 1996), *Los Locos* (Vallée, 1997), *Naturally Native* (Farmer & Red Horse, 1998), *The Hi-Low Country* (Frears, 1998), *Seraphim Falls* (von Ancken, 2006), *3:10 to Yuma*, *Appaloosa* (Ed Harris, 2008), and Ang Lee's two Westerns for Focus Features *Ride with the Devil* (1999) and *Brokeback Mountain*.

The contemporary wave of independent Western production is not new to the sector. A huge number of Westerns were produced by the independent Poverty Row companies (such as Monogram and Republic Pictures) from the 1930s to the early 1950s. However, the uses of the genre for a more overt and didactic political questioning is typical of a post -1960s independent cinema.[14] Finally one could also detect the revisionist impulse in certain studio Westerns after the 1960s, such as John Ford's *Cheyenne Autumn* (1964), but these have remained rather rare occasions.

Film Genre and the Western

In 1953, in the title of one of his two essays on the Western, the French film theorist André Bazin referred to the genre as the American film *par excellence*.[15] The Western is, after all, about America, the founding of the nation, a particular version of history, and the epic story of the making of its people as (white) Americans. In 1953, the year of Bazin's essay in French, the Western was an important American cultural export screened in bulk as part of the postwar Marshall Plan. Following Bazin, the Western assumed a central place a decade later within the history of Anglo-American film studies and the development of two key conceptual frameworks, genre criticism and film authorship. Both approaches emerged in the mid- to late-1960s with the British Film Institute's Cinema One publications of Robin Wood's *Howard Hawks* and Jim Kitses's *Horizons West*.[16] The Western was one of the first film genres to undergo the kind of analytical work that was once reserved for other humanities-based academic disciplines (in its infancy film studies was framed by literary conceptualisations of its object, namely through the author and the text). *Howard Hawks* and *Horizons West* were among the first of several influential books to establish cinema as a serious object of scholarly inquiry and analysis and perhaps less obviously, the study of popular culture. The seriousness and scholarly rigour of *Howard Hawks* and *Horizons West* in tandem with the translation and publication in English of a steady number of writings from France contributed to the gradual institutionalisation of Anglo-American film studies and helped legitimate the discipline in universities throughout the 1970s. The Western was foundational to such an establishment and once framed through scholarly approaches to genre and authorship, it was subsequently placed as a disciplinary progenitor of sorts. Specifically, Kitses and Wood's studies were followed a few years later by John G. Cawelti's *The Six-Gun Mystique* (1971) and Will Wright's *Sixguns and Society* (1975).[17]

In *Horizons West* Kitses takes up the then influential model of analysis called structuralism. The structuralist methodology was broadly adapted from the work of French anthropologist Claude Lévi-Strauss.[18] Lévi-Strauss's structural anthropology argues that social and cultural meanings depend on a series of oppositional structures. These structures give rise to mythologies which are the beliefs of a particular society and culture. A basic mythology of the classical Hollywood Western is that the cowboy is good and the 'Indian' is bad. The cowboy/Indian opposition in which the latter is demonised produces a contemporary myth that helped legitimate the real historical colonial expansion and genocide of indigenous Americans. A binary logic also underpins structuralism which subsequently lends itself well to texts. It is especially suited to genre as generic structures are often formulaic in their apparent working of thematic and visual oppositions.

Indeed, genres (like the Western) by their very nature present an easily identifiable repetition of key elements and pleasures such as the saloon brawl, the frontier encounter, or the gunfight. Kitses's borrowing of Lévi-Strauss's work reveals how genres can be easily understood as the cultural artefacts of a society. Westerns correspond to the notion of a mythology through the plethora of ways in which, as genre texts, they repeat with reliability their aesthetic and ideological meanings through identifiable thematic and stylistic oppositions. *Horizons West* and *The Six-Gun Mystique* present the Western as an inherently structural form, a system of meaning with a very specific organisation of oppositions (wilderness versus civilisation, freedom versus restriction, cowboy versus Indian), repeated visual elements (guns, Monument Valley), thematic underpinnings (cattle drives, rescues, building communities, tracking down outlaws), and an archetypal set of stock characters (the cowboy, the outlaw, the saloon girl, the Indian chief). Kitses's central argument is that the Western articulates a 'philosophical dialectic, an ambiguous cluster of meanings and attitudes that produce a traditional thematic structure for the genre'.[19] Kitses begins by outlining a series of antimonies or structural oppositions to support his analysis. Wilderness versus civilisation is the main antinomy from which the other subsumed oppositions commence. These antimonies have been cited many times as a key example of the structural design of a film genre, while the methodology itself can be applied to qualify other genres such as science fiction with its oppositions between human and alien, and nature and technology. It is instructive to provide an abbreviated selection of Kitses's antinomies here, as they are presented in *Horizons West*:[20]

The Wilderness	**Civilisation**
The Individual	The Community
Freedom	Restriction
Self-knowledge	Illusion
Integrity	Compromise
Nature	Culture
The Frontier	America
The Past	The Future

In the Western, the central tension is between the wilderness and civilisation which can be reduced to a more readable (and familiar) opposition between the frontier desert and the town. The narratives of the Western have both emphatically and obliquely recounted the story of progress and expansion to build communities and instil laws (*Red River* here is a good example) through the loss of the wilderness and the way of life it celebrates, which is characterised by adventure and lawlessness. The antinomies suggest a more rigid conceptualisation than what the Western adheres to and there is a reductive impulse to read this as a strict either . . . or binary logic. However, Kitses himself is quick to suggest there is more flexibility in the Western genre when he describes it as a 'loose, shifting and variegated genre with many roots and branches'.[21] It would seem that Kitses is implicitly acknowledging that film genre in general, and the Western in particular, both conforms to and challenges its own definitions and canonicity. Kitses mentions Gene Autry (the singing cowboy) and Roy Rogers as his canon-defying examples.[22] His suggestion is ever so brief, only a few sentences in a paragraph, but I see his mention as a sort of caution against the belief in some essentialist core to the Western and for the concept of film genre as an inherently monolithic structure.

John G. Cawelti's *The Six-Gun Mystique* continues to invest in structuralism. Cawelti introduces similar concepts in myth, formula, convention and invention, and adds to the mix Marxism and psychoanalysis in order to make sense of the Western as a hegemonic form, a cultural entity that is common sense, at once both psychic and social. In his analysis Cawelti also places importance on textuality and he teases out the ideological undercurrents produced through settings and topographies. He suggests how the *mise en scène* orchestrates 'conflict between civilization and savagery' and functions as 'an effective backdrop for the action'.[23] Therefore, Cawelti's emphasis on how the Western looks, the grandeur of its spectacular landscapes, the details in the *mise en scène*, and the ways in which the characters behave and act (particularly the cowboy's verbal reluctance), all of these, he argues, vie to organise the meaning of the genre as a mythic-ideological form. Interestingly, Cawelti too cautions against a kind of interpretive essentialism of genre in remarking that 'the Western's capacity to accommodate many different kinds of meaning' is what makes the formula so successful.[24]

Both *Horizons West* and *The Six-Gun Mystique* and Will Wright's *Sixguns and Society*[25] imprint the study of the Western with a rich array of ideas and interpretive frameworks linking the textual and the ideological. Many of the foundational arguments and observations are expanded upon and reiterated in more nuanced forms throughout the substantial body of scholarship devoted to the Western. This is especially important with regard to history, race, gender and the representation of the West in a diverse array of cultural contexts and mediated forms. In addition to studies on the Western as an essentially American film genre, the valuable work on the Italian Western helps to further problematise and challenge many of the assumptions claimed for the Western as an exclusively American cultural form.[26] The way in which the Italian Western is expunged from nearly all studies of the Western actually makes the European variation a strong ally for thinking about the Western and otherness, as both are somewhat known to be part of the Western yet deliberately avoided or disavowed. Both 'spaghetti Westerns' and 'gay cowboys' put the nation at stake by making manifest, on the one hand, the arbitrary nature of national identity, and on the other hand, the place of same-sex desire in history.

Brokeback Mountain as a Western

Normally, in order to qualify as a Western, a film is usually set in a particular historical moment roughly between the Battle of the Alamo in 1836 and the Mexican Revolution in 1913. With its story beginning in 1963, *Brokeback Mountain*s seems to come far too late by historical definition.[27] Yet, the impression we are given by the film is of an American milieu that otherwise represents a continuum with the old ways and values of Western life, albeit drastically altered by twentieth-century capitalism but seemingly unchanged by twentieth-century ideology. If *Brokeback Mountain* is not set in the distant past of the epic moment it certainly evokes and clings on to the mythology of the West: the figure of the reticent cowboy; his unique attire; the solitary lifestyle; rodeo culture; farming and working with animals; the homestead and its restrictions on men's freedom; the power of the wilderness and nature; nostalgia invoked through country and western music. Because it begins in 1963, *Brokeback Mountain* might not represent the West as an epic moment and its ranch hands might not be considered real cowboys. However, I would argue that *Brokeback Mountain* represents the elided history of homosexuality in the context of a continuum with the West. I would also argue that *Brokeback Mountain* represents a West that survives through the cultural traditions, practices and ideologies of specific US regions associated with Western mythology. *Brokeback Mountain* is set between Wyoming in the north-west and Texas in the central south. In this context, the West is still mythic, an imagined fantasy, a discursive construction, a concept of a way of life that, I am suggesting, we understand to be presented in the film as an unbroken continuum with the West of the past.

The dialectical relationship between wilderness and civilisation is readily apparent in *Brokeback Mountain*'s rather obvious thematic and aesthetic oppositions between freedom and restriction, the mountain and Riverton. *Brokeback Mountain* typifies the Western through its obvious structuring of life in the wilderness, symbolised through Jack and Ennis's freedom to love one another there, and in opposition there is the civilising pull, the reality of small town life with their respective wives and children, compelling the men to conform to a failed heteronormative existence. What makes *Brokeback Mountain* unique in relation to the dialectic is that these major antinomies are frequently unstable, reversed, transversed, and ultimately queered. Note the Germanic origin of the term queer is *quer*, which means to cross, adverse and make oblique. In this respect, one could suggest that the antinomies are not entirely subsumed within the film's major structuring opposition between the freedom of same-sex desire in nature and the restrictions of a compulsory heterosexuality regulated through socialisation and the family. The latter actively depends on homophobia, repression and the closet. It is possible to see how the Western, with its valuing of the freedom of the wilderness and the all male kinships, is almost engineered to support a neat slippage from a cowboy's homosocial camaraderie to an enactment of his homosexual desire.

In addition to this, *Brokeback Mountain*'s near contemporary setting and the ideology underpinning the liberal politics that inform the 2005 film actually criss-cross in a queer way the wilderness/civilisation antinomy and are less stable than the true binary whose logic depends on a forceful gulf between incompatible forces. There are numerous oppositions in *Brokeback Mountain* and it is these adaptations from Kitses' original structuralist model that allows one to consider the film as a queering of the Western rather than a simply a movie about gay cowpokes. Being queer, these additional oppositions refuse to adhere to a straightforward regulation of one side and the other. Rather they are messier and potentially rhizomatic, as queerness (as in queer theory and the queering of the Western) is inherently destabilising and deconstructive in its practice. For instance, the difficulty in pinning a sexual identity on to Jack and Ennis (if sexuality is not defined solely by their sexual acts) and their inability to know their own identity as potentially gay men (and to specify what that means for them) already suggests an antagonism between different forms of hetero and homo categorisation as these relate to assumptions about masculinity and femininity in the Western genre. Further oppositions (discursive, sliding, alternating, overlapping) that we might add to a shakily structured binary are between the queer and the normative, the homosexual and the heterosexual, the couple and the family, freedom and the closet, and secrecy and disclosure. In anticipation of the analysis it should appear that these oppositions are obvious in their connection to Kitses's model as wilderness readily collapses freedom and homosexuality into one another. However, this manoeuvre needs to be further qualified through a concrete linkage with queer theory, specifically in relation to Eve Kosofsky Sedgwick's important work *Epistemology of the Closet*.[28]

Sedgwick argues that the opposition between homosexual and heterosexual definitions, categories and identities also informs and organises the way we make sense of, and produce knowledge about a range of other binary oppositions such as public/private, secrecy/disclosure and masculine/feminine. For Sedgwick the entire epistemological framework of Western thought and being, especially when it pertains to knowledge about identities and desires, hinges upon a central distinction between heterosexual and homosexual difference. The organisation of these oppositions works in order to maintain a hegemonic position for heterosexuality through an anti-homosexual production of knowledge, of which homophobia and the closet are two such forms. The whole gamut of oppositional structures that Sedgwick details informs how 'culture' allows its people to *know* homosexuality (as an epistemological formation) through the ways homosexuality is frequently collapsed on to one side of a binary in opposition to a heterosexual norm (reminiscent of the classic example of defining identity as the self through the other).

What is understood about culture and identity is informed by the distinctions drawn from the major categories of heterosexuality and homosexuality which are produced through forms of surveillance, regulation and policing not just by the others of our binary but also by ourselves. Think, for example, of Ennis's paranoia. The maintenance of difference, through forms of knowledge and processes of knowing from the cultural to the medical, is central to the political and ideological separation of homosexuality and heterosexuality as primary markers since both are mapped out in relation to other sets of meaningful oppositions that include same/different, private/public, masculine/feminine, knowledge/ignorance, majority/minority, natural/artificial, and health/illness.[29] *Brokeback Mountain* explodes how many of these distinctions' adherence to one another operates both generally, as a production of knowledge about identity, and specifically, through film genre as a system of regulation. Heterosexuality's self-definition is an effect of homosexuality's alignment with concepts of minority, illness, artificiality and secrecy which all seem to readily collapse in on one another.

The policing of sexuality through the conceptual-ideological apparatus of the binary maintains a heterosexual agenda of normal and natural definition but also points to the instabilities and constant threshold of rupture that would seek to reveal the artifice of heterosexuality as culturally, epistemologically and discursively produced. That Jack and Ennis are 'regular guys' is for many an anxiety inducing wake-up call that homosexuality is frequently non-indexical and non-stereotypical. The enforcement of hetero/homo distinctions is precisely an effect of their instability and this is what *Brokeback Mountain* draws attention to: moments of rupture and the indelibility of sexual definition as it brushes against the generic formula of the Western's own categorisations of meaning in which homosexuality has for the most part been excluded or sublimated. In *Brokeback Mountain* the rigidity through which sexuality comes to be known and understood by its protagonists is shown to be forced through the dynamics of the closet and homophobia. Yet, the film also shows us the undoing of heterosocialisation through the relationship between masculinity and homosexuality in men who appear to be 'straight' cowboys. Furthermore, the relationship between sexuality and gender is unmoored in a film genre that has historically been part of the very institutional and regulatory processes of meaning to produce knowledge about normative genders and sexualities in the first place.

What *Brokeback Mountain* actually offers is a competent illustration of Sedgwick's argument in *Epistemology of the Closet* as it complements the troubled binary that has framed the Western's initial formulation. Like all genres, the Western is by definition an episteme in that it engenders the production, constitution and reception of forms of knowledge. This might be as simple as the film audience's expectations to see gunfights and spectacular arid vistas and not two men getting cosy in a tent. As a cultural form the Western has often sought to regulate the knowledge of a particular version of American history, a selective and corrupted version of historical knowledge as well as particular accounts of sexuality predicated on constructions of masculinity, assumed to be heterosexual, standing in opposition to a side that includes in its zone of meaning femininity, emotion, culture and domesticity. *Brokeback Mountain* overturns this epistemic production and attends to the classic Western's often immutable relationship to its own binary logic by, for example, bringing domesticity to the wilderness through Jack and Ennis's campsite and by positioning homosexual desire on side with nature, 'manliness' and freedom. I would ask the reader to bear Sedgwick in mind throughout the analysis of *Brokeback Mountain* and its relationship to the multiple binaries that orbit it.

Wilderness, Landscape, Freedom

The wilderness is conjured by the title *Brokeback Mountain*. It is a fictional place created by Annie Proulx to represent 'isolation and altitude' but also as an 'empowering and inimical' place.[30] The mountain also symbolises the one place in the film where Jack and Ennis are able to enact on their desires unrestricted and momentarily free from fear, shame and paranoia. Brokeback Mountain comes to symbolise a sort of freedom, a temporary escape from the closet, and the film values this through an investment in the landscape. Brokeback's splendour is visually and thematically figured in opposition to the bleak claustrophobia and drain of small town family life. Other critics, however, interpret the same construction of the wilderness in different ways. For instance, in his discussion of *Brokeback Mountain* Jim Kitses views the construction of the landscape as one of isolation and loneliness.[31] The paradox of reading *Brokeback Mountain*'s backdrop of visual grandeur as potentially representing both freedom and isolation problematises Kitses's own earlier antinomies. Wilderness versus civilisation, as the film makes clear, is never a straightforward opposition between a liberating freedom and depressive restriction typical of the Western as both antinomies bring with them a slew of problems primarily associated with the men's closeted status. Neither the wilderness of Brokeback Mountain nor the small town community offer long-term solutions, happiness or a path to lifelong love. Ennis is as much isolated by his shame and paranoia at home as he is isolated by the expanse of the mountain range.

However, *Brokeback Mountain*'s investment in the wilderness and the rural does play an important role in challenging the frequent alignment of homosexuality with urbanity, a term of conflation that Judith Halberstam neatly coined as metronormativity.[32] *Brokeback Mountain* fictionally accounts for those rural gay and lesbians, however troubled by their context, whose histories and experiences unfold away from the big city and modernity. This challenges the metronormative myth that informs contemporary gay and lesbian experience whose trajectory often recounts the tale of the rural queer coming to the more inclusive city as the means to enable their coming out experience. If the Western has expunged the homosexual then the opposite might be also said of queer cinema which by and large has rejected the rural. Alternatively, the rural context that makes *Brokeback Mountain*'s Jack and Ennis's homosexuality so difficult to realise suggests that the two protagonists do not see the lure of freedom that the city often represents as an option (as has been the case in more conventional homosexual narratives of self-discovery).[33] In *Brokeback Mountain* the wilderness is thus cast as a potentially contested space that represents both freedom and isolation.

The cinematography of *Brokeback Mountain* brings in to sharp view the breathtaking outdoor scenery, even if Alberta in Canada stands for an absent Wyoming. In the film there are frequent and lingering shots of the mountain vistas and the natural spectacle, seductive and powerful in producing an intoxicating and affective topography that evinces a desire to imagine being there as much as Ennis and Jack's desire is to escape there too. One could suggest, then, that structures of desire in the film seem to operate in a circuit between the awe-inspiring visual spectacle of landscape, which invites spectators to overinvest in it, and the desire the men have for each other. This becomes even more clear in the scenes when the two men are separated from each other, which signify for the spectator the (temporary) denial of access to the pictorial landscapes that give us so much pleasure. The spectators are often reminded of the fact that Ennis and Jack's relationship was built on Brokeback Mountain, with the final get-together scene between the two protagonists poignantly emphasising that Brokeback Mountain is 'all they got'. The only time we ever see the men truly happy is during those moments spent in the wilderness, on horseback, and around the campfire on their 'fishing trips'.[34]

Indeed, Jack and Ennis's relationship takes place almost entirely outdoors, except for one tender scene in a dimly lit motel. Within the mythology of the Western, masculinity – much like the two men's homosexuality – is conveyed through the burdenless freedom of outdoor life, one that appears to be free from the conformity of civilisation, its laws, practices and regulatory discontents. Like many other Westerns before it, *Brokeback Mountain* claims the landscape and the frontier for its symbolic meaning to express freedom and the cowboy's affiliation and closeness to nature, the land, and of course to the other cowboys who might be out there too.

Ang Lee, Judy Becker (the film's production designer) and cinematographer Rodrigo Prieto worked together researching and designing the visual look for *Brokeback Mountain*. Perhaps surprisingly, given the

Figure 1 Wilderness in *Brokeback Mountain* (© Focus Features)

existence of such large numbers of Westerns to draw ideas from, several of their reference points for the landscape were the iconographic representations of the West in American twentieth-century art. These include the lighting and composition of Edward Hopper's paintings, the landscapes of Andrew Wyeth, and more importantly for screen aesthetics, the landscapes and people photographed by Ansel Adams, William Eggleston and Richard Avedon.[35]

In March 2006, *Interview* magazine's *Brokeback Mountain* cover story featured Michelle Williams alongside a career retrospective portfolio of Bruce Weber's photography entitled 'The cowboys in my life'.[36] Weber's portfolio renders clearly his ongoing homoerotic fascination with the West in a career that would seem to be built on a (homo) eroticisation of rural America as innocent and uncomplicated. Weber's photos suggest how homoerotic images of ranchers and cowpokes work to memorialise masculine beauty, implying that there is inseparability between images of Western masculinity and homoeroticism. Weber and the other three mentioned American photographers (Adams, Eggleston and Avedon) have been celebrated for their ability to capture the myths and textures of the West in their photographs, in bodies of work that are mediated by a distinct undercurrent of nostalgia. Landscape and masculinity are two of the most potently symbolic elements in the Western because their visual power so readily translates geographical spaces and bodies into epic mythologies and concepts of freedom. And the photographic images by these artists succeed in conveying these symbolic elements as natural, timeless and beyond the buzz and pressure of urban and metropolitan cultures. This is also echoed in *The Six-Gun Mystique*, when Cawelti suggests that the topography of the Western has the 'tendency to elevate rather commonplace plots into epic spectacles' and 'helps to dramatize more intensely the clash of characters and the thematic conflicts of the story'.[37]

Brokeback Mountain's visual power would not have had such a hold if it had been entirely set in an urban milieu, partly because there are numerous queer films that have already presented similar stories in the context of the city. Representations and stories of homosexuality in rural and small-town contexts are all too rare and *Brokeback Mountain* sits alongside *Boys Don't Cry* (Pierce, 1999), *The Laramie Project* (Moisés Kaufman, 2002), and the upbeat *Big Eden*, which is set in Montana, as queer films that eschew the already mentioned solidifying alignment between homosexuality and the city. It is precisely because *Brokeback Mountain*'s protagonists seem to be cut off from civilisation and the politics of postwar America that the dialectical structure of the Western holds such power in narrating the drama of homosexual desire and repression through the tension inherent in the Western's visual and thematic oppositions. In other words, the significance afforded to the landscape as a symbolic element in *Brokeback Mountain*'s overall meaning is one where the wilderness itself becomes representative in expressing homosexual desire as something naturally occurring. The investment we have in the landscape also works as a metonymy for the tragedy of the situation in which Jack and Ennis eventually lose each other. Their relationship is related to the spectator's gradual loss of the landscape, eventually reduced to a mere postcard on the closet door of Ennis's caravan.

Civilisation, Restriction, Domesticity

In contrast to *Brokeback Mountain*'s wilderness, the setting that conveys civilisation, town and community is often drab, miserable and claustrophobic. It evokes little positive feeling. This is after all the place that produces the closeted and repressed desires of its cowboys. Cinematographer Rodrigo Prieto explains in an interview for *American Cinematographer*:

We wanted to visually separate the men's everyday lives in Wyoming, where Ennis lives, and Texas, where Jack lives, from their experiences on Brokeback

Figure 2 Civilisation in *Brokeback Mountain* (© Focus Features)

Mountain', says Prieto. 'For day exterior mountain scenes, I used [Eastman EXR 50D) 5245 because I wanted those images to feel a little crisper and cleaner – I wanted the air to be more transparent'. Daylight scenes down in the towns were filmed on Kodak Vision 250D 5246 to achieve 'a touch more grain and a touch more contrast', he continues. 'Judy Becker's production design featured muted colors, and we wanted [the town] to feel a little grayer, a little harsher than the mountain scenes.[38]

The different film stocks create aesthetic and textural differences that enable the genre's structural antinomies to be easily read through visual style. The most extreme interior in this respect is the home of Ennis, which is often filmed with very low-level lighting. This lack of light and its direction through the dingy windows of his house indicates a general state of depression and confinement. (In these examples, this Western film clearly makes use of *mise en scène* conventions that have been firmly associated with the genre of melodrama, and Chapter 3 offers a detailed discussion of the film as melodrama.) The dominant colour palette is muted and lifeless with hues of brown and grey. The messy arrangement of furniture and props also implies a cluttered and impoverished life with Ennis trapped in a marriage that, the *mise en scène* suggests, is a life wasted away in stuffy confinement (see Figure 2). The small town of Riverton and Ennis's chaotic house function as one gigantic visual code for repression. Ennis lives in misery as a victim of internalised emotions that he cannot find words to express. His ideological naivety, hard graft and poverty, in tandem with his efforts towards a heteronormative life, are further exacerbated by the screaming children that dominate the diegetic soundtrack.

Jack is economically better off than Ennis and his domestic setting is, in contradistinction, neither claustrophobic nor depressing. Jack's home is not stuffy and muted by lifeless colours; instead, it is pictured as unloving, conveyed through tensions with his wife's family, petty social appearances and obligations. He is situated in a life which is measured and valued by the standards of economically determined social mobility and patriarchal authority. Jack's private space of domesticity with Lureen and the public space of work are deliberately muddied, to the extent that the division between the tractor showroom (where Jack works) and the home are never ascertained. The majority of conversations and marital interactions between Jack and Lureen take place in the small office at her father's business rather than in the privacy of home. Their existence is equally unhappy but for different reasons than the ones identified for Ennis. Jack's emotionless life in Texas is also aided by the *mise en scène*, which works to convey isolation and disconnection. The homes of both Jack and Ennis represent the obstacle to their happiness and the ideological force of the family as a social organisation works to quell the mere existence and possibility of a gay life as one of their options.

Home is often a contested space in queer experiences. It is often not the place of safety and belonging and is instead a space of conflict and homophobia that one escapes from. Jack and Ennis are both unable to fulfil their desires, despite Jack's efforts to persuade Ennis to build a home together, unsuccessful even after his divorce from Alma. Domesticity and town life, as the civilising forces of the genre, help to define in contradistinction a freer life outdoors that is characterised as inherently more appealing. The town is about settling down and quelling the adventure, male camaraderie and cowboy way of life. Cawelti's discussion of the town makes it easy to imagine where Jack and Ennis's homosexuality is positioned within such a claim:

The town offers love, domesticity and order as well as the opportunity for personal achievement and the creation of the family, but it requires the repression of spontaneous passion and the curtailment of the masculine honour and the camaraderie of the older wilderness life.[39]

'Love, domesticity, and order' take on a characteristic hue in *Brokeback Mountain* namely, as heteronormativity. The exertion of normative social forces and expectations that make heterosexuality the only option for Jack and Ennis stand in opposition to the temporary respite that Brokeback Mountain offers as a place to escape to. The Western's antinomies are even more clearly articulated as they map sexuality on to discourses of wilderness and civilisation. Jack and Ennis's sexuality is repressed by social expectations of home which destroy them both. Their love for one another is only occasionally and briefly enacted upon in the only place that remains unhindered and beyond surveillance. Like in the classical Hollywood Western, the wilderness is the space left untamed by social forces. In *West of Everything*, Jane Tompkins describes how the West functions symbolically, and in turn how *Brokeback Mountain* might be viewed in relation to the wilderness, in bringing together a sense of escape with the fulfilment of desire. As she puts it:

The West functions as a symbol of freedom, and the opportunity for conquest. It seems to offer escape from the conditions of life in modern industrial society; from mechanized existence, economic dead ends, social entanglements, unhappy personal relations, political injustice. The desire to change place also signals a powerful need for self-transformation.[40]

Tompkins's discussion of civilisation is also a fairly accurate description that translates *Brokeback Mountain*'s queer politics. A central argument in Tompkins's book is that the gendered logic of the Western positions the wilderness versus civilisation antinomy as one related to gender. This position echoes Sedgwick's argument and reveals how hetero and homo definitions also become relevant ways of making sense of other types of distinctions, especially in terms of gender. The Western produces knowledge in its gendering of wilderness and civilisation but in *Brokeback Mountain* this is re-imagined through sexuality. Like Packard in *Queer Cowboys*, Tompkins mainly focuses on Western literature from the period and makes a strong case in arguing that the genre's masculine bias 'answers the domestic novel' and 'is the antithesis of the cult of domesticity that dominated American Victorian culture'.[41] In the Hollywood genre the feminised contexts of domesticity are cast as an anathema to the cowboy who is caught between the desire to love and settle down with a female companion – usually a nice schoolteacher rather than a saloon floozy – or continue his outdoor adventures with his male comrades. As a mythic structure this is one issue that Westerns attempt to resolve despite our knowledge that civilisation inevitably wins.

The opening scene of John Ford's *The Searchers* (1956) is the most obvious example of the Western's gendered logic that organises meaning on both a thematic and visual level. It is repeated in countless variations throughout the genre and, interestingly, is somewhat echoed in *Brokeback Mountain*'s portrayal of Alma. In the famous opening scene of *The Searchers* the camera is placed in a position that stages the first shot as coming from inside the home. The camera tracks from behind an as yet unidentified woman who emerges from the interior darkness to open the door that leads out to the sun-blazed frontier. Moving onto the porch to gaze upon the scorched panoramic expanse of Monument Valley, she eventually catches in her sight the slowly emerging figure of the cowboy who seems to come from nowhere. He appears to materialise from the landscape itself. More family members emerge from the home and stand on the porch to witness the return of the cowboy Ethan (John Wayne). This sequence from *The Searchers* seems to place a lot of emphasis on the woman and her family not setting foot off the porch, as if an invisible force has drawn a line between the frontier and the home. This shot/reverse shot pattern allows for a neat alternation between the ranch and the landscape creating the ideological opposition through markers of visual difference. This opposition between frontier and homestead is additionally coded through light and dark, cowboy and family, placing masculinity, nature and freedom on one side of the binary and femininity, culture and the home on the other.

The scene in *Brokeback Mountain* that seems to reproduce this logic of gendered opposition is Jack and Ennis's first reunion. This scene is also discussed in Chapter 4 in relation to spectatorship. In this scene, Alma secretly watches from a vantage point from inside the home as Jack and Ennis embrace and kiss outside in a stairway nook. Alma's immediate response is to quickly close the door in a reversal of the opening of the door in *The Searchers*, as if to shut out the unthinkable and let it happen in a place beyond the confines of the home. This clearly suggests that she wants to keep their homosexuality out in the 'wilderness' where it apparently belongs. This scene marks an opposition between home and outdoors, inside and outside, a division we can also understand to crisscross the opposition of homosexual and heterosexual. Alma rarely leaves the confines of the home, like the woman in *The Searchers* and in countless other Westerns, except on a few occasions when she goes to work in the local grocery store in Riverton. Alma remains anchored to a number of domestic meanings that the film, through its *mise en scène*, characterises as downtrodden, gloomy and drab. One could argue that the *mise en scène* makes us feel sorry for Alma and it often works in conjunction with the narrative to solicit an empathetic reaction from the spectator.

This means that *Brokeback Mountain* often uses two conflicting and complicated positions of identification between male homosexuality and female heterosexuality and it frequently defers to the distinctions drawn between the outdoors and the home. However, the spatial mapping central to the Western's ideological thrust is complicated by *Brokeback Mountain*'s queering of the antinomies. For example, before Jack and Ennis do meet each other in the scene described above we almost always see Ennis at home or with the family. When Ennis first waits for Jack he is seen looking out of the window from a position inside the home much like the passive 'waiting woman' of melodrama described by Mary Ann Doane.[42] Jack barely enters Ennis and Alma's home, opting instead to stay in the hallway close to the door as if he has wandered too far already.

When viewing *Brokeback Mountain* through Kitses's antinomies it is important to stress that the film is not constructing a conservative ideology of gender that reduces and fixes gender to tropes of wilderness and civilisation. *Brokeback Mountain* actually complicates and even contests the antinomies by having gender and sexuality encroach on each other's binary. It is the deconstructive impulse of the film's queering of the Western that is at work here. Both genre and gender are being exposed in the film through assumptions and definitions of homosexuality and heterosexuality and their relationship to Western conventions and formulae. Think, for instance, of the way in which the campsite slowly transforms into a space of domesticity for Jack and Ennis. Here domesticity is no longer distinct from the wilderness but is in fact part of the wilderness as the outdoors is refashioned into a makeshift home. This domestication of the wilderness becomes a queer alternative to the heteronormative home and additionally offers spectators an alternative way of reading the development of Jack and Ennis's relationship – through the *mise en scène* rather than dialogue. As Jack and Ennis draw closer to one another the campsite comes to represent their intimacy through its homeing.

Unlike more traditional and stereotypical Westerns such as *The Searchers*, *Brokeback Mountain* plays out the opposition of wilderness and civilisation less strictly and more thoughtfully in relation to sexuality, which is inseparable from gender anyway, and offers a strong case for the film's queering of the genre through the means of film style.

Masculinity, Talk, Emotion

Actions speak louder than words. This is a mantra when it comes to certain American film genres and their construction of masculinity. Representations of masculinity and emotional reticence are often allied to a strong silence in men.[43] For the cowboy, it would seem too that reticence is one instance of how masculinity gets constructed in relation to silence, introspection and mystery. Masculinity becomes invisible and unknowable because men in movies do not talk about being men. Too much talk can be revealing and can lead to emotions. Such resistance to feeling in the Western and in other genres allows the creation of another gendered division in that men tend to remain silent and taciturn unless there is something meaningful to say: an order, facts, an observation, or a piece of wisdom for the younger cowboy in tow. Cawelti notes that the 'reluctance with words often marks the hero's reluctance with women'.[44] This in turn suggests that superfluous conversation and exposition, especially too much talk, are aspects that only concern the feminine spheres of influence. Here, again, we see another opposition. The patriarchal assumption prefers to think of women's conversation and talk (and also that of homosexuals) as merely gossipy, inconsequential and trivial.

Although the Western is not the only film genre to sign up for this particular construction of masculinity and the taciturn hero, save for those smart one-liners, it is nonetheless the one genre whose currency and agency always revolves around the body rather than speech, and actions as opposed to emotions. The Western is the one genre where men talk only when they have to and *Brokeback Mountain* apes this convention of the taciturn cowboy portrayed in the mumbling and tight-lipped performance of Heath Ledger's Ennis. Ennis's inability to articulate his emotions through language are damaging to himself and others and his frustration quickly turns to anger and violence because he lacks the means to vent his feelings in any other way. In one scene he nearly hits Alma for bringing up the 'fishing trips' with Jack Twist, or as she calls him 'Jack Nasty'. Alma's insinuations compel Ennis to confront the homosexuality he cannot find words to describe. The use of language in the film also reveals the construction of class separating Ennis and Alma from Jack and Lureen. As Tompkins notes:

Western heroes don't have the large vocabularies an expensive education can buy. They don't have time to read many books. Westerns distrust language in part because language tends to be wielded most skilfully by people who possess a certain kind of power: class privilege, political clout, financial strength.[45]

Ennis does not speak much throughout the film and at times it is difficult to understand what he says as he talks through a clenched jaw and pursed lips. (Amy Villarejo actually makes a point about the film's particular fascination with Ennis's jaw.[46]) As the years pass, it is Jack who makes suggestions for a change in their life and Jack who poses questions about their relationship and future, while Ennis remains tight-lipped. Even the film's narrative seems to make a knowing comment about Ennis's difficulty in articulating his thoughts. In an early scene, and while around the campfire on Brokeback Mountain, the first verbal exchanges between Jack and Ennis take place. Ennis begins to recount some of the stories from his past, prompting Jack to comment: 'friend, that's more words than you've spoken in the past two weeks', to which Ennis immediately replies 'hell, it's the most I've spoken in a year'. The film constructs its cowboys with an awareness of the role that conversation or lack of it plays in their life and the gradual opening up of Ennis through his stories about the past is a sign of growing intimacy. As Ennis is not able to say how he really feels about Jack, and would not be the first to act upon his feelings in the first place, he asks Basque to bring the tins of soup that he knows Jack prefers instead of beans. This is Ennis's non-verbal gesture of affection. The tins of soup are just one example of something taking the place of speech for Ennis.

Ennis becomes the latest addition to a long list of screen cowboys whose 'silence symbolizes a massive suppression of inner life' with a 'determined shutting down of emotions'.[47] This often leads to the cowboy's undoing and eventual loneliness. In *Brokeback Mountain* the silence of Ennis is more than just a trait of his Western masculinity and lowly social status; it is more importantly the silence of the closet, the quelling of desire and the feeling that homosexuality is not something that can be properly expressed either to himself or even to those closest to him. Sedgwick writes that 'closeted-ness, itself is a performance initiated as such by the speech act of silence'.[48] One could argue then that *Brokeback Mountain* draws attention to silence as a queer issue and not just a masculinity and Western issue. *Brokeback Mountain* takes the figure of the taciturn cowboy and reinvents him as the conflicted figure of an inarticulate homosexual desire not just out of time (in 1963) and out of place (in rural Wyoming) but also out of words.[49] Ennis seems to prefer silence, and Heath Ledger turns out a memorable performance as the quiet cowboy who stumbles over his words. However, it is Ennis's closeted homosexuality that underlies the silence of the silent cowboy whose desires find other outlets for expression. Traditionally, this inability to express oneself has been displaced onto violence in the Western and violence is certainly something that Ennis is prone to. However, such anguished phrases in Ennis's lexicon as 'I wish I knew how to quit you', were quickly assimilated into the parlance of popular culture in ways that mock the emotional resonances of the film. Heath Ledger's portrayal of the inarticulate Ennis, a man unable to deal with his own homosexuality, connects reticence to the damage enacted by the closet whose foundation lies in silence. In this sense, *Brokeback Mountain* queers the genre convention of the taciturn cowboy.

A Queer History of the Western

At the 2006 Academy Awards, the year in which *Brokeback Mountain* took its three Oscars, there was a montage of scenes from Hollywood Westerns. The host John Stewart ironically presented the montage to the audience with the quip that 'there's nothing gay about the classical Hollywood Western'. In a series of very quick extracts from numerous films the following is implied: men's interest in other men's guns is sexual; guns are inherently phallic and penetrating, especially when fondled and thrust into other men's faces; editing also helps to recast a series of quick scenes of undressing and gun belt removal as male striptease; looking relations between cowboys, again a trick of editing in the montage, is marked by longing and desire rather than hostility; bestiality and pederasty are also part of the West, after all is homosexuality not just another perversion? What this montage achieves is not an unveiling of the Western's homosexual or queer subtexts. Instead, the effect of editing, along with Stewart's opening and closing framing of the montage, actually works to render such readings of the Western as somewhat ludicrous. Interestingly, the montage did not include any butch women like Joan Crawford and Mercedes McCambridge from *Johnny Guitar*, nor did Doris Day's famous tomboy from *Calamity Jane* feature, nor any number of Westerns featuring Barbara Stanwyck magnificently butched-up.

The same desired effect, to render the possibility of queerness and homosexuality in relation to the Western ludicrous, was also achieved by David Letterman's *Brokeback* response 'Ten Signs You're a Gay Cowboy' on *The Late Show with David Letterman* (CBS, 1993–).[50] Among Letterman's list there were: 'you love riding but don't have a horse'; 'instead of a saloon you prefer a salon'; 'your saddle is Versace'; and a number of other references which discursively construct gay cowboys as effeminate, fashion obsessed and musical-loving. In other words the gay cowboy becomes another instance of impossibility, this time through the act of stereotyping. Letterman's list actually depends on the same gendered logic of the classical Hollywood Western in which the cowboy's macho self-fashioning as heterosexual is defined through its opposition to sissification. In this respect, feminisation and domesticity are wholly rejected in favour of certain regulatory alignments.

Along with these mainstream media responses to the film, the expanse of serious criticism on the Western from monographs to edited collections, especially those not undertaken by gay and lesbian scholars, has often cast the structure of male–male desire as one gigantic blind spot. Gay, lesbian and queer analysis of the Western is to be found in books that do not take the Western as their main focal point and thus rarely threaten to intervene on the genre's apparently heterosexually-inflected interpretative exclusivity.[51] Yet, homosociality is at the heart of the genre's male camaraderie and is certainly not so far down the line of the continuum from its bedfellows, homoeroticism and homosexuality.[52] In Westerns men do not love each other, in the sense of being homosexual or romantically involved (although it can be this too), but rather they share strong bonds and deep friendships. The Western as a film genre is full of these male pairings and couples, relationships so often dependent upon the problematic exclusion and expulsion of women and men as rivals for any additional affections and attentions that may break certain idealised pairings. As Vito Russo once asked in relation to *Butch Cassidy and the Sundance Kid* (George Roy Hill, 1969),'who remembers Katherine Ross?'[53] The Paul Newman and Robert Redford pairing in *Butch Cassidy and the Sundance Kid* is often hailed as an example of an idealised couple with a homosexual undercurrent emanating from the stars' chemistry.

Homosexuality has long been the secret of the Western and the more distant from the classical cinema we get, the more its disavowals become less concealed. Reception practices have always demonstrated that homosexuality cannot be simply read between the lines as that would imply there is a correct 'straight' way to read a film prior to an aberrant queer reading. The interplay of connotation and denotation has been the primary means to reify homosexuality in Hollywood cinema as something both simultaneously seen and unseen. The entire point of *The Celluloid Closet* is to reveal this slippage between connotation and denotation that both Vito Russo's book and the documentary rather simplistically reduce to good versus bad representations.[54] In what follows I want to examine two Westerns, the classical Hollywood *Red River* and the contemporary indie remake of another classical Western, James Mangold's *3:10 to Yuma*. Both films contain elements that we would deem homosexual and/or homoerotic and feature characters whose homosexuality is surreptitious and covert (Matthew Garth in *Red River*) or clearly discernible and flaunted (Charlie Prince in *3:10 to Yuma*). As a caveat I have restricted myself to the discussion of just two films, a classical and a contemporary, and two films that relate specifically to male homosexuality rather than homosexuality in general, which would include lesbians. *Calamity Jane* and *Johnny Guitar* are two of Hollywood's queerest Westerns but I want to refrain from bringing them into a debate about male homosexuality and homoeroticism for fear of reducing the specificity of a discourse that would otherwise rob the lesbian pleasures and meanings. However, *Calamity Jane* and *Johnny Guitar* cannot go unnoticed and I would draw the reader to the excellent queer analysis of those two films in the footnote.[55]

A Brief (and Personal) Note: The Western and Gay Cinephilia

Given the Western's quotient of male display and camaraderie, it is arguably surprising that the genre has not produced the kinds of gay cinephilia reserved for other classical and contemporary Hollywood genres, especially the much loved musical and the melodrama. On the other hand, though, the iconography of the Western has consistently kept alive a homoerotic visual currency across many other aspects of gay culture, from fashion (the enduring checked and plaid shirts) to all manner of soft and hard pornographies. In this respect, *Brokeback Mountain* would seem to respond to the gay cinephile's oversight by actually placing a Western film within a broader spectrum of Western-themed fantasy that has hitherto been permeated by the assumption that mainstream or Hollywood Westerns and gay spectators were mutually exclusive; or that this specific Hollywood genre has been untouched by the forces of gay cinephilia and film fandom.[56] A revealing and assumptive comment about audiences is made by Douglas Pye in his *The Movie Book of the Western* when he refers to the 'appeal of the genre *for male audiences*' [my emphasis].[57] From a queer point of view, this kind of statement also masks the normative tendency to understand the category of 'male audience' with a certain vague and universalising implication that elides in its generalisation the assumed straightness of the male spectator of Westerns.

Furthermore, assumptions about the audience for Westerns as being a straight man's genre convey resistance to negotiating the gay and lesbian subtexts of the genre. To take my own experiences as an example, my formative queer cultural development, absorption and subsequent rejection of gay male cultural expectations (the inbuilt tutelage of gay culture's likes and dislikes), in which film played a central part, did not include any Westerns or even the idea that it was a film genre I should be watching as part of my emergent gay identity. This might have been simply generational, as plenty of openly gay film scholars, including Robin Wood and Steve Cohan, have written intently about the Western, while if I had seen films like *Johnny Guitar* (Ray, 1954) as a teenager I might have recognised that there was something queer there. I also implicitly understood – in a naive way – that Westerns (and one could add, among other things, heavy metal music, racing cars and football) were not elements of gay culture, which is strange given the eroticisation of the cowboy in gay culture that I would later find occupied a prominent space in fantasy. On the other hand, it was an expectation, if not requirement, that some degree of familiarity with those other Hollywood genres (like the melodrama and the musical) would lend some importantly needed gay cultural capital.

One could argue, then, that, like Andy Warhol's *Lonesome Cowboys* (1968), gay men's interest in the Western was more of an attachment to a look than it was a commitment to a genre. For this reason, *Brokeback Mountain* has allowed me (and I suspect a lot of other gay men) to develop a belated interest in the Western genre, albeit without losing sight of our allegiance to queer thinking and the problems and pleasures the Western poses for gay men's histories of popular culture interaction and formations of spectatorship (see in particular Chapter 4).

Re-viewing the Western

Patricia White's concept of retrospectatorship is instructive in helping us to make sense of a re-reading of the classical Hollywood Western. It is *Brokeback Mountain* that prompts us to re-view the classical Hollywood Western 'that belongs to the past but is experienced in a present that affords us new ways of seeing'.[58] *Brokeback Mountain* as a contemporary Western helps shape a retrospective reading of older Westerns, particularly examples like *Red River* that have either struggled to disavow their homoerotic underpinnings or have made obvious a range of queer possibilities. Re-reading the classical Western with this objective in mind is not necessarily an appropriating practice or even a subversive re-imagining of a particular articulation of the genre. Instead, as Alexander Doty has suggested, it is a questioning of its default position, which clearly has taken straightness as its organising principle.[59] This position has been greatly supported by the creation of heterosexual couples and the patching together of generic and romantic closure at the end of countless films and has worked to proffer a 'preferred reading', quite simply because we have all learned to 'think straight' in a way that secures such reading.[60] In this respect, *Brokeback Mountain* seems to have answered the call to all those elided and hinted at stories of same sex desire in the Hollywood Western by retrospectively prompting a return back to older films from a vaulted position of contemporary spectatorship. *Brokeback Mountain* engenders a privileging of being able to un-think assumptions about Westerns in relation to sexuality. As Patricia White brilliantly demonstrates in her re-reading of classical Hollywood, our spectatorial vantage point as queer subjects is steeped in knowingness about how Hollywood edited out homosexuality and cast it to the realm of the connotative;[61] while D. A. Miller suggested that the eliding of homosexuality's denotation 'exploits the particular aptitude of connotation for allowing homosexual meaning to be elided even as it is also being elaborated',[62] which explains how homosexuality by its very absence is made meaningful throughout classical Hollywood cinema.

There are a number of informed analyses of classical Hollywood Westerns that re-view the genre and the films' construction of masculinity and relations between men as both homoerotic and homosexual. These analyses elucidate a queerness in the text that the passing of time has made more easily recognisable, so much so that, arguably, the 'straight' reading ought to be subtextual. In their readings of Western films, Creekmur, Cohan, Farmer and Lang all reveal the homoerotic dynamics and 'masculine interests' that are central to the Western genre.[63] Homoeroticism, in particular, is a term that is frequently used by all authors yet it has almost always escaped definition. Homoeroticism is characterised as a response to or fascination with the image of men, as either producer or consumer, that is experienced as pleasurable and erotic. Obviously this is particularly privileged as a form of pleasure for gay men. Identifying and experiencing the homoerotic has something to do with recognising the mutual fascination men have for each other, yet it is difficult to explain the frisson that it often provokes. Richard Dyer has provided the fullest account of the concept, which is worth quoting in some length:

> Homo-eroticism tends to stress libidinal attraction without sexual expression, sometimes even at the level of imagination and feeling. While in some usages homo-eroticism can be a wider term which includes homosexuality, or can be a euphemism for homosexuality, it importantly indicates a sense of male pleasure in the physical presence of men, or even sometimes in their spiritually or ethically masculine qualities, which cannot be contained by (or, discourses of homo-eroticism would tend to say, reduced to) the idea of queerness.[64]

Dyer's suggestion that homoeroticism 'indicates a sense of male pleasure in the physical presence of men' comes very close to describing the Western's appeal for men, gay or straight, as the genre can be considered as perhaps the most masculine of all genres. Cawelti's description of the cowboy in *The Six-Gun Mystique* conveys his own homoerotic fascination – 'boots, tight-fitting pants or chaps, his heavy shirt and bandana, his gun and finally his ten-gallon hat' – a description that produces a fantasy image, especially through Cawelti's need to place some emphasis on the tightness of the cowboy's pants.[65] The Western is a homoerotic genre because its investments are rooted in the visual pleasure of male display – spectators looking at the cowboy and cowboys looking at each other – prompting Robert Lang to go as far as identifying a 'homosexual voyeurism at the heart of the genre'.[66]

Indeed, the Western narratives that frame the cattle drives and the frontier adventures are routinely couched in the dramatic relations between men and the confrontations and rivalries that operate among male pairings and groupings. Creekmur's reading of *My Darling Clementine* (Ford, 1946) points to the way in which Henry Fonda and Victor Mature's first encounter in the saloon reads like a pick-up in a gay bar: glancing, cruising, buying a drink and so on. The pick-up argument is further supported later in the film by dialogue, cinematography and *mise en scène*, all working to suggest there is much more to this famous cowboy pairing than the narrative would otherwise suggest. Of course, this does not necessarily mean that all cowboy pairings in the Western can be read in this way but on the other hand there is a list of examples from the genre where the homosexual undercurrents make very strong appearances, including *Red River*, *Johnny Guitar* and *Calamity Jane*, while the documentary based on Vito Russo's *The Celluloid Closet* (Epstein and Friedman, 1995) also adds *Butch Cassidy and the Sundance Kid* to the above pictures.

Arguably, the homoerotic Western *par excellence* is Howard Hawks's *Red River*, a film in which a good deal escapes the cloak and dagger 'shadow kingdom of connotation'.[67] A contemporary viewing of *Red River*, armed with the knowledge that one of its central stars, Montgomery Clift, was a gay man, provides the insight that White's retrospectatorship makes so persuasive. The spectator's first introduction to Montgomery Clift's Matthew Garth character is startling in its invitation to look at his handsome boyish looks. Standing aloof he seems to be gazing down towards John Wayne's crotch while sucking on a piece of straw. The camera cuts from the medium shot to a close-up of Clift's face as he looks towards Wayne. This instantly constructs him in relation to a relay of desiring looks: the spectator's look at him and his look at Wayne. Thomas Waugh suggests that 'for homoerotic culture in particular, the gratification in/of looking seems especially important, as it is for other stigmatized "perversions" because looking not only stimulates and organizes desire but also legitimizes it'.[68] In the facial close-up Clift looks on, tonguing the single piece of straw that dangles from his mouth as Figure 3 shows.

The shot of Clift's face seems to linger for an extra beat but it is the minor details (the piece of straw, the tongue and the open mouth) that a queer reading of Clift's body and performance values. Such minutiae jump out retrospectively as signifiers of Montgomery Clift's queerness. He plays with a delicately phallic piece of straw in a way that hints and suggests sex, an oral tease, which is undeniable in its capacity to be read as homoerotic. Retrospectators are now left wondering how much of Clift's homosexuality infiltrates his performance as Matthew Garth.

In a more general vein, Steve Cohan discusses Clift's performance in *Red River* and describers how the star 'uses physical gestures to draw attention to his presence in a shot, rubbing his face, caressing his nose, holding his chin, sitting side-saddle on his horse', to the extent that it 'implies Matthew's passivity as erotic spectacle'.[69] Cohan's reading of the film emphasises 'the trope of boyishness' in Montgomery Clift in

Figure 3 Montgomery Clift in *Red River* (1948) (© United Artists/MGM)

contradistinction to the rugged manliness of John Wayne as the film sets out, leaving the rest of the narrative to work through the opposition between the soft boy and the hard man.[70] It is Clift's performance of boyish passivity and its theatricalisation of erotic passivity, Cohan suggests, that typified a new type of postwar masculinity, which arguably found its best exemplification in the characters portrayed by James Dean. Clift's softness in *Red River* helps to define his erotic appeal and Cohan points out that it is precisely this aspect of his performance that challenges the hegemonic forms of masculinity as those are typified in the film by John Wayne and his star persona.[71] The passivity, softness, sensitivity and boyishness of Clift emphasise the sexuality of the cowboy. These are the non-phallic attributes of cinematic masculinity, which are described by Brett Farmer as being particularly 'receptive to gay identificatory investments'.[72] Farmer also suggests that Clift's effeminacy is characterised in the way his body and good looks are treated in a similar way to the conventions of cinematic femininity in classical Hollywood. Clift is coded as spectacle through close-ups and soft lighting, which is how the first shots of his face in *Red River* appear.

If this straw-chewing shot of Clift is not convincing enough to queer his performance and this particular example of the Western genre, there is another scene in *Red River* that has prompted even more attention to the connotative power of reading Clift's gayness in the film. This scene is also early in the narrative and involves Garth and rival gunslinger Cherry (John Ireland) comparing guns and having a shooting match. What should, in fact, be a routine scene in a Western becomes a barely hidden attempt to eroticise the coupling of the young cowboys in clearly suggesting the pistol-as-penis. Garth and Cherry fondle and size each other's guns then shoot a tin can as if they were 'adolescent boys engaged in mutual masturbation'.[73] The brief exchange of dialogue that sets up this 'I'll show you mine if you show me yours' scene is as follows:

Cherry: That's a good looking gun you were about to use back there. Can I see it?
[Matthew turns, thumbs his nose and looks a bit surprised, then hands his gun over. Cherry takes the gun]
And you'd like to see mine.
[Cherry draws his own gun and passes it to Matthew. Cherry examines Matthew's gun]
Nice! Awful nice! You know, there are only two things more beautiful than a good gun: a Swiss watch or a woman from anywhere. You ever had a good Swiss watch?
Matthew: Go ahead! Try it!
[Matthew points to a tin; both fire at it and hit it]
Cherry: Hey! That's very good!
[Both shoot at another can]
Matthew: Hey! Hey! That's good too! Go on! Keep it going![74]

At the start of this exchange, Matthew thumbs his nose and looks downward when facing Cherry, the way he did earlier in front of Dunston (Wayne). It's a coy and coquettish gesture in Clift's performance that is playful in terms of him being a tease, suggesting the passivity that his gunplay will in fact deny. They swap guns and begin a shooting contest. The can pops in the air with each other's alternating pistol shots with a vertical logic and intensity one might associate with ejaculation. As a matter of fact, Robin Wood has, indeed, called this 'the scene of cruising, mutual masturbation and ejaculation'.[75] This scene recalls the earlier moment, shifting emphasis from the piece of straw to Matthew's gun. The middle part of the dialogue also needs some commentary as it seems to bear the burden of the scene's homosexual overtones in stressing a Swiss watch and a woman from anywhere. This reads as a quick, almost defensive posturing akin to 'I'm not gay but . . .' that in its very need to be spoken actually makes the queerness of the scene more evident than had it not been scripted. It works like connotation in the same way that Miller has suggested. The elision of what is obvious (homosexuality) actually elaborates more emphatically on its very absence.

The scene is also important in setting up a rivalry between Matthew and Cherry but the film never stages the confrontation that the narrative anticipates and unfortunately we never get to know if the future includes any 'cherry popping'. Wood and Cohan both view this omission as the consequence of this scene's homoerotic set-up and point to a general consensus in the dangling cause that has puzzled viewers of the film since. There is no Matthew/Cherry development in *Red River*. Cohan sees this as an isolated moment of spectacle in the film that functions like a number in the Hollywood musical. It only appears as a 'self-contained moment of erotic spectacle' even when the dialogue hints at a future showdown.[76] Wood, on the other hand, sees the omission of any future development between Matthew and Cherry as the authorial choice of Howard Hawks's own anxieties to curtail the development of a relationship that this scene clearly sets up as both homoerotic and homosexual.[77]

As a more recent example of a Western, the Lionsgate remake of *3:10 to Yuma* (the original was directed by Delmer Davis and was released under the same title in 1957) demonstrates that homosexuality demands its place in the Western. The new *3:10 to Yuma* confirms the homosexuality of the Charlie Prince (Ben Foster) character and his love for the outlaw Ben Wade (Russell Crowe). The film enacts its own process of retrospectatorship in its reading back of the original to upgrade homosexuality from connotation to denotation. It is tempting to view the emphasis on Prince's homosexuality in the remake as a nod both to the genre's open secrets as well as to *Brokeback Mountain*'s making fashionable the homosexual cowboy. The remake makes it clear that Charlie Prince is a queer and Byron McElroy (Peter Fonda) even calls him Charlie Princess in an early scene, as if to establish this fact. Although Prince's homosexuality is not hinted or a secret, one still has to know how to read the signs in order to understand the way in which looking and performance are structured to render homosexuality materially present. Prince is dressed differently (the cut of his leather jacket is more precise; it is tapered at the waist; he has more cowboy accessories), which makes him look more stylish and dandified than the other cowboys. He carries his body in a different manner too as, for instance, occasionally leaning his wrists on the butt of his holstered guns. He also does not think twice about shooting men in the back and he kills the hero Dan Evans (Christian Bale) this way. Prince is cruel and sadistic but shooting a man in the back goes against the ethical code of a fair and noble, manly face to face shoot-out. In this respect, it is tempting to read Prince's homosexuality as further coded in his preference for 'taking men from behind'. This is also slippage into reductive and clichéd assumptions that only views male homosexuality through a rear logic.

D. A. Miller's analysis of *Rope* (Hitchcock, 1948) is instructive here. In Hitchcock's film a number of the concealed cuts in the film take place on men's backsides, and Miller's analysis of the editing, in a film about two homosexuals it never names as such, suggests how connotations of homosexuality in the cutting make a textual and structural allusion to the dark recesses of the anal.[78] Even the design of one of film posters for *3:10 to Yuma* positions the viewer kneeling at the behind of Prince instead of the more conventional picture of Christian Bale and Russell Crowe's faces. When the film was released Charlie Prince was accused of being yet another retrograde example of American cinema's homophobic representation of queer villainy who, like all the other queers, ends up dead in the end.[79] However, I would like to argue that Prince is far from being a retrograde stereotype of yesteryear and, instead, can be read as the uncompromising figure of the homosexual outlaw that Leo Bersani would champion as anti-communitarian and anti-normative.[80]

As a secondary character, we never really find out much about Prince, except that he is equal parts style and sadism, but the film does make a point of allowing the character to take control of his own gaze, one often marked by an equal measure of desire and disappointment in his love for gang leader Wade. The cowboy's desire is never acted on in terms of sexual relations; rather, their unionisation and the basis for their intimacy and closeness is conventionally displaced onto violence and criminality. There are a few pivotal scenes that mark the desire between the two outlaw cowboys: one early in the narrative that takes place in a saloon and one towards the end when Wade kills Prince for shooting *a tergo* Dan Evans. In the saloon sequence Prince looks up at Wade who in turn is gazing at the barmaid whom he eventually takes upstairs. The relay of looks here, Prince looking at Wade and Wade looking at the barmaid, mirror each other in terms of desire for the object of affection, but the hetero-centric pull can only ever confirm the normative position that will couple Wade and the barmaid (let us not also forget that Wade is played by Hollywood megastar Russell Crowe). In this sense, Prince cannot do anything else but leave, articulating his disappointment through the delivery of the line 'I'll wait for you'.

Like many Westerns before it, the film gives us the ideal couple in two cowboys, only to pull back and confirm heterosexual coupling as the only real possibility while still hinting at the potential of something equally plausible. Spectators have to imagine when Prince leaves the saloon disappointed that he has at least been taken 'upstairs' on occasion having been the object of Wade's affections in the past. Prince's attachment to Wade is continually emphasised, obvious in his loyalty to the gang and Wade as the dreamy counter-shot of his point of view. It is also in the small details such as Prince's reclaiming of Wade's stolen hat and revolver. Prince makes a point of getting his lover's precious items back in order to offer them to him as a gift. A connection between clothing and desire is established in this small detail that echoes the symbolic place that Jack and Ennis's cowboy shirts also occupy. The final scene between Prince and Wade absolutely confirms their relationship as being built on both a romantic and a criminal coupling but also carries a tragic dimension as Wade's chivalrous code necessitates that he must kill Prince for shooting Dan Evans from behind. Wade kills him for the betrayal of literally taking another man from behind.[81] Wade holds Prince close to him as he is dying and in a close-up of each character's face, structured as a shot/reverse shot similar to that which would be used for two lovers in the cinema, the film confirms their love, as tears begin to well in Prince's eyes. But almost immediately their future is denied as Wade puts a final bullet straight into Prince's heart: a death fitting for a criminal lover. Typical of the Western, the recent *3:10 To Yuma* confirms desire among cowboys only to eventually rebound, deny it any future, and render it fatal.

Independent Westerns: The Queer Westerns of Andy Warhol and Bob Mizer

In the 1960s the classical Hollywood Western was in decline, with fewer productions and less critical attention, which was also indicative of waning audience interest. The 1960s also witnessed a shift towards a different type of popular cinema and film stardom that reflected social revolution and civil rights as well as an emergent second wave feminist and gay and lesbian politics. The stoic conservatism of John Wayne was out and the short-lived rebellion of James Dean was in. Production figures of the Western throughout the decade rarely reached double figures even though the decade saw the release of many notable titles like *Cheyenne Autumn*, *Hud* (Ritt, 1963), *The Outrage* (Ritt, 1964) with *Butch Cassidy and the Sundance Kid* and *The Wild Bunch* (Peckinpah, 1969) closing the decade. It was around that time that production of the Western shifted to Italy where the Italian film industry made its own variation to satiate the popularity among local audiences for a genre that Hollywood no longer seemed to produce in bulk. The invention of the 'spaghetti Western' was symptomatic of the dearth of Hollywood Westerns in the 1960s.

Despite this decline in mainstream Hollywood productions of the genre, 1960s American cinema did engender a different kind of take on the Western, one that was rooted in gay cultural production. This completely independent to Hollywood, alternative production (and reception) context was located in two areas, the New York underground cinema and the Los Angeles-based mail order physique culture. These two contexts are important because they confirm an alternative history of the Western that makes no apologies for the homoerotic fascination that it stirs. The appeal of the Western scenario and the figure of the cowboy in these gay contexts openly acknowledge and exploit to an elevated degree what is already present in Hollywood examples of the genre. *Brokeback Mountain* belongs to this alternative history of the Western that finds its antecedents not only in classical examples like *Red River* but also in the 1960s leftfield underground films of Andy Warhol and the clandestine 16mm productions of Bob Mizer. Warhol and Mizer's films make even more explicit the erotic appeal of the Western and the cowboy for a gay male audience, emphasising further the already existent homosexual undercurrents. Furthermore, these films also appeared several years before the Oscar-studded *Midnight Cowboy* (Schlesinger, 1969) confirmed to its hip counter-culture audience that the cowboy look was really 'fag's stuff', and therefore stand as ground-breaking examples of a truly independent cinema. Ironically, as it turns out, gay culture and the independent sector were two of the few cultural contexts of America in the 1960s within which the cowboy actually still had some real currency.

Andy Warhol made two films that could be loosely called queer Westerns. The first one was entitled *Horse* (1965) and the second and better known one, *Lonesome Cowboys* (1968).[82] As a queer artist Warhol had already celebrated the homoeroticism of the Western in his iconic Elvis screen print (*Double Elvis*, 1963). The Elvis prints reproduce a publicity image from one of his lesser-known films, a Western called *Flaming Star* (Siegel, 1960). Richard Meyer's reading of the 'homoerotic mirroring' of Elvis as a cowboy makes an important point with reference to the repetition of the image of the cowboy printed next to one another, overlapping in a position that 'activates the erotic possibility of man-on-man contact'.[83] *Double Elvis* also marks Warhol's fascination with Hollywood stardom that gets filtered through his queer sensibility. A great deal of Warhol's 1960s output responds to the centrality of popular cinema and stardom in American life and pre-Stonewall gay culture.

There is also a noticeable range of engagements with Western iconography in his work. These include: a very early camp illustration of a horse coloured with purple ink (*Horse*, 1950); late career screen prints of John Wayne, Geronimo and Annie Oakley (from the aptly titled *Cowboys and Indians* series, 1987); the polaroids and screen prints of Dennis Hopper in his cowboy hat (*Dennis Hopper*, 1977); various guns (*Guns* series, 1981); and the Howdy Doody puppet (*Howdy Doody* series, 1981) taken from the Western-themed children's television show of the same name. Arguably, Warhol's most revealing in its homoeroticism Western-related work is an early pre-pop illustrated spread from 1957 called *Crazy Golden Slippers*. The double-page spread that appeared in *Life* magazine features imaginary footwear for the likes of Zsa Zsa Gabor and Truman Capote but among them is a gold cowboy boot for James Dean and Elvis Presley.[84] The fantasy boot for Dean is described on the page by Warhol himself as a 'James Dean inspired squirrel Western boot to convey a rugged character'. Coded in this phrase is the erotic desire not just for James Dean but that for the cowboy in general as a 'rugged character', that is, the erotic appeal of the 'rough trade' masculine man and his gear, epitomised in the cowboy boots.

Warhol's first 'Western' *Horse* was filmed on 3 April 1965 and is typical of his 16mm film period that includes other single word titled films such as *Empire* (1964), *Kiss* (1963), *Sleep* (1963) and *Eat* (1963). *Horse* is a sound film, three reel-long, black and white, a single shot set-up, lasting 100 minutes.[85] For the production of the film Warhol rented a horse that was brought up to the Factory in the service elevator, was sedated and then filmed alongside four typically handsome Factory boys dressed as cowboys.[86] In Ronald Tavel's script they are called Mex, Tex, Sheriff, and the Kid. The cowboys interact with each other, teasing and flirting, camping it up, cavorting and fooling around, posing, and generally annoying the horse with pretend zoophile affections.

Ronald Tavel calls *Horse* 'a deconstructed Western'.[87] The first of Tavel's scenarios depicts the cowboys fooling around, accusing each other of murder while The Kid suggestively strokes and kisses the horse. The second scenario is a step outside the genre with the horse being fed by its owner. This was filmed after and inserted between the two 'performed' reels. In the third scenario the cowboys are playing strip poker down to their jockstraps; they then fool around with each other until a tape recorder plays back a rendition of *Faust*. To the uninitiated this all might seem absurd and far removed from the idea of a Western but this is underground cinema! Tavel's script clearly indicates how several scenarios culled from the Western (accusations of murder, a horse, petty cowboy rivalries, a downtrodden Mexican, poker) offer a natural set-up to stage a series of homoerotic games. What *Horse* perhaps suggests is the true meaning of 'horseplay': the justification for how rough and rowdy play among men, whether in the West or not, enables them to legitimately come into close physical contact with one another. Furthermore, the title *Horse* probably alludes to penis size through the popular phrase 'horse hung' (as it was common knowledge among his associates that Warhol had a soft spot for well-endowed men).

In reel one the Sheriff accuses Tex and the Kid of murder then the Kid makes advances on Tex who is spurned. This in turn makes Tex jealous when he starts undressing the Sheriff. Reel one is also replete with scripted lines that form the basis of deliberately clichéd dialogue such as 'there's gold in them there hills' and 'all this land is gonna be mighty fine cattle country' in addition to innuendos like 'my gun is my tool' (a line that immediately recalls the phallicisation of Montgomery Clift and John Ireland's gun play in *Red River*). The dialogue is often at odds with the image, as is typical of Warhol's sound features, matching well-worn Western phrasing to blatantly homoerotic images. The image of *Horse* produces a conflict that perhaps suggests that the Western's narrative and dialogue (which Warhol's film renders banal) is at odds with the image which cannot contain the truth of the cowboy in his capacity to be unavoidably homoerotic. Through the parody of recognisable scenarios *Horse* merely teases out the homo-ness of what belies the Western's own dedication to male–male relations, while its aping of generic conventions produces mini narratives that are homoerotic and merely provide the catalyst for a homosexual parody of the Hollywood genre. *Horse* responds to the fact that the genre and the cowboy possess a ready-made homosocial and homoerotic context for a queer reconstruction.

If very few spectators have seen *Horse* then the opposite can be said of Warhol's *Lonesome Cowboys*. The latter is perhaps more fully realised as a Western as it takes place in an old movie set, but is arguably less interesting than *Horse*'s more experimental reworking of the genre. Originally to be called *The Unwanted Cowboy* and then *Ramona and Julian*, *Lonesome Cowboys* is also the film that initiated an FBI investigation of Andy Warhol. The FBI tried to prosecute Warhol for 'interstate transportation of obscene material', crossing state lines with his 'dirty' Western.[88] Furthermore, *Lonesome Cowboys* has also attracted the most attention, both in terms of critical accounts of the film and, interestingly, in terms of criticism of these accounts, which have often been divisive in relation to whether the film has any merit as a retrospective queering of the Western.[89]

Lonesome Cowboys was filmed in a small town called Oracle near Tucson, Arizona, on a Western movie set that was initially built in 1939 for the film *Arizona* (Ruggles, 1940) and subsequently used in many other Westerns.[90] The film drew tourists to Warhol's shoot, originally there to see the filming of conventional Westerns (probably the television series *Death Valley Days* [1952–75]), but who eventually became fixated by Warhol's 'one woman all-fag cowboy town'.[91] According to Steve Watson it was one of the onlookers, a 'concerned parent', who logged a complaint that piqued the FBI's interest in Warhol.[92]

It is easy to read the complaints and moral outrage along with the FBI investigation as homophobic, a direct response to Warhol's defilement of the Western. Warhol recounts a tourist's outburst of 'You fags! You Queers! I'll show you who's the real cowboy around here, goddamn it!' and how the Factory were run out of town by the technicians employed on the movie set.[93] Like the homophobic responses to *Brokeback Mountain*'s 'rape of the Marlboro man', there is an anti-gay sentiment that views these films as an attack on the sanctity of the Western and it further supports a thesis that aims to explore what goes unsaid in the Hollywood Western. *Horse*, *Lonesome Cowboys*, and *Brokeback Mountain* are films that merely confirm what the Western already contains yet keeps suppressed, namely the relationship between homoeroticism and same-sex desire.

Lonesome Cowboys was one of the few commercially released Warhol films and is one of his most widely seen features. The film is pieced together out of a series of homoerotic and camp vignettes premised on the arrival of a group of cowboys in a Western town that culminates in a rather uncomfortable-to-watch rape of the Warhol superstar Viva. The film is still typical of the Western in that it reproduces a binary opposition between the outlaw cowboys and the good townsfolk but also articulates an uneasy opposition between heterosexual and homosexual masculinities, between camp and butch queens. As with many of the Westerns discussed in this chapter, *Lonesome Cowboys* attends to the 'breakdown of the Western genre in the face of its previously unarticulated homoeroticism'.[94]

Criticism of *Lonesome Cowboys* is almost as difficult to digest as the film is to appreciate and the analysis that attempts to make sense of *Lonesome Cowboys* runs circles around the contradictions in the relationship between masculinity, homosexuality and genre. Richard Dyer has suggested that *Lonesome Cowboys* is 'less coherent and critical conscious' than the interpretations imply.[95] Peter Gidal was the first to offer sustained commentary on the film and despite its sexy cowboys and outré homoeroticism he claimed that the film was 'sweet' and 'not erotic'.[96] Dyer's comments, partly a response to Gidal, characterise the film's deconstruction of the Western as defying analysis but still goes on to outline the film's exploration of masculinity and the desire for the image of male beauty that *Lonesome Cowboys* solicits in its furnishing of a homoerotic gaze.[97] However, Dyer views *Lonesome Cowboys* as a text that works against the potential of the film to generate any critically conscious sense of real pleasure for the gay spectator. This is because *Lonesome Cowboys* fails to resolve its critique of the Western and cannot confirm whether it values the butch manly man of the 'real' Western who potentially usurps the camp figure of the 'queer' Western.

Matthew Tinkcom has added to the amassed criticism, arguing that *Lonesome Cowboys* is 'not a simple substitution of queer male desire into the form of the (apparently) masculine Western'.[98] Tinkcom values *Lonesome Cowboys* more generally for its experimental approach to cinematic sexuality and gender, reading retrospectively the film as a queer text through the indelibility of masculinity. This is a point that finds Dyer agreeable as, despite his criticisms, he has applauded the film's knowing construction of masculinity as a performed set of codes and conventions.[99] One of Tinkcom's claims is that the violence perpetrated against Viva in the rape scene is a critique of the Western's wholesale repression of homosexuality and the 'value' that it affords to masculinity per se. He also makes an important observation that reflects directly on the interpretation of *Brokeback Mountain*'s construction of masculinity when he suggests that 'the problem of whether these figures deserve the name of "real men" is related to questions of the *value* afforded to masculinity in the Western'.[100] In other words, it is the fact that *Brokeback*'s Jack and Ennis are by all accounts 'real men' (bodies that are culturally read as straight) that creates the homophobic reactions of disbelief, both in the story and in the audience.

If Warhol represented the experimental and avant-garde end of gay cultural production in the 1960s then Bob Mizer represents in opposition a form of moviemaking that was more accessible (in an aesthetic sense) and commercial, though always independent from mainstream filmmaking.[101] Both Warhol and Mizer were drawn to the homoeroticism of the Western but with different artistic outcomes and intent. Mizer's vision of the West and the cowboy was entirely fetishistic and drew on the appeal of the cowboy and his gear as a figure of 'real' masculinity. *Physique Pictorial* and the countless other physique magazines throughout the 1950s and 1960s, such as *Vim, Adonis, Drum, Muscles, Vigour, Tomorrow's Man, Body Beautiful* and *Rawhide Male*, were mass culture publications that openly sold healthy 'beefcake' images of nearly naked and fully naked young men, oiled and surrounded by various props, under the guise of classical aesthetics, body building, fitness and health. Wrestling was a particularly favoured theme of physique culture since it legitimated bodily contact offering unique positions from which to view the interlocking of male bodies. A quick glance at the magazines suggests an artist's innocence in the appreciation and study of physical athleticism but a closer look at the smaller details reveals the more clandestine operation behind the magazines. Many of them served as the basis for a more lucrative mail order service through which readers could purchase much more revealing photo sets of models, without obligatory posing pouches, and with coded information about their sexual practices and preferences. From 1958 onwards Mizer began producing 8mm and 16mm movie 'loops' for private viewing, including the projectors to play the films, all delivered to the home in plain brown boxes.[102]

Christopher Nealon characterises the early postwar physique culture as a 'public secret' since the magazines were widely distributed on American newsstands, openly parading homoerotic images of masculinity for all to see while simultaneously disavowing the relationship of these images with homosexuality, let alone a vast homosexual readership.[103] The physique magazines existed because the mindset of the 1950s and early 1960s was one that viewed homosexuality through effeminacy and gender inversion and not in any way related to images of healthy, happy and muscular boys and men. The Hollywood Western's own homoeroticism works in a similar way, namely that images of a cowboy like Matthew Garth in *Red River* were adversative to what was conventionally understood as homosexual. For Nealon, physique culture makes 'explicit the pleasures of displacement' through a closeting discourse that reneges with force both femininity and gay sexuality in its production of homoeroticism.[104] This closeting of gay sexuality in the reception of physique culture echoes the Western genre's own disavowals at the pleasures men take in each other and is precisely what films like *Lonesome Cowboys* and *Brokeback Mountain* make no qualms in fully disclosing. Countless covers, illustrations, and photo spreads in the physique magazines and films included cowboys and Western settings from the fully decked Western *mise en scène* to only a few gestural props such as cowboy boots, holsters, and ten gallon hats as maximum naked male flesh was the *sine qua non* of the magazines' visual economy.

These photo shoots also became film reels when Mizer began producing his mail order films. As little of Mizer's film output is publicly available for analysis (even the Internet Movie Database lists only two films by the filmmaker), I will only refer to two short films he made during his later period (the late 1960s). The films *Nevada Smith Posing* (1969) and *Jealous Cowboys* (1970) differ from one another, not in terms of how they present the beefcake body but in terms of the mode of address they adopt, which positions the spectator differently. In the narrative film *Jealous Cowboys* the spectator is a voyeur, privy to an altercation between two jealous cowboys, while in the posing film *Nevada Smith Posing*, the spectator is a participant who is privileged by an exhibitionistic display that directly engages them.

In *Nevada Smith Posing* the title of the film, a reference to the model's pseudonym and his posing act, first appears in block letters next to a gun. This sets up the Western context of this four minute long film. Nevada Smith walks in from a door to the left of the frame, already naked except for his cowboy hat, boots, holster and gun. He looks straight at the spectator and says 'Howdy'. He then begins posing for the next few minutes facing front on and then turning to each side in a typical mishmash of bodybuilding poses and cowboy stances. Part of the posing is the drawing of the gun in and out of the holster and its directing towards the audience as if to shoot them. Eventually he yawns, which also signals a change in position as he lies down and falls asleep, just as the film ends. The posing and the different positions of the body from standing to lying are designed to maximise the flopping of the flaccid penis from as many angles as possible. This type of film was also called a 'danglie' for this reason. However, what makes this short film interesting is the reduction of the Western to a few key props and the threat posed by the gun as it targets the audience. *Nevada Smith Posing* stretches the Western in terms of genre but it presents the cowboy as a homoerotic fantasy and his gear as fetish objects. The *mise en scène*, which is minimal and more than likely filmed in Mizer's home, also includes a sizeable statue of Michelangelo's David that often appears in the background right of the frame. The cowboy joins Michelangelo's David with the pretence of drawing comparisons between classical aesthetics and soft-porn beefcake, Michelangelo and Mizer, but also suggests a teleological history of homoerotic subjects.

When Nevada Smith draws his gun and shoots at the spectator (see Figure 3) it conjures up an amusing analogy in its references to *The Great Train Robbery* (Porter, 1903). *The Great Train Robbery* is considered one of the first movie Westerns and the film's most well known shot, its last shot (which is almost a coda to the narrative), is a shot of the cowboy pointing his gun at the spectator and shooting (see Figure 4).[105] In Mizer's film, the threat of violence directed at the audience is a means of circumventing the spectator's unproblematic taking of Nevada Smith as the passive object of their gaze. In this respect, the relationship between the subject and object is not typical of commercial cinema since the power involved in looking and display is never fixed. A different way of reading Nevada Smith's direct look at the spectator is as a male pin-up. Richard Dyer suggests that the male pin-up confronts those who would take him as their object through a gaze that either ignores or challenges the spectator. This stands in contradistinction to the 'come hither' look of the female pin-up of 'cheesecake' who invites the gaze through the erotic passivity coded in her body.[106] *Nevada Smith Posing* presents a contradiction in its exhibitionist display, one whose purpose is to solicit the erotic pleasure of consuming the male body, especially muscles and penis, in addition to the fetishistic props that invoke the Western. Yet, the spectator is almost dared to do so through the threat of violence. *Nevada*

Figure 4 *Nevada Smith Posing* (1969) (© AMG)

Figure 5 *The Great Train Robbery* (1903) (© Kino Video)

Smith Posing offers a play on active and passive, looker and looked, that may or may not be seen to progressively challenge the imbalances in erotic spectacle and spectatorship normatively reified through male and female. *Nevada Smith Posing* may actually suggest, if we are to read it as a Western, that passivity when confronted by a rugged cowboy's threats is one of the genre's secret pleasures. Physique culture's preference for sadomasochistic forms of male bonding is, as Thomas Waugh suggests, one that works to produce a position for the spectator whose fantasy is that of a bottom role.[107]

The erotic switch point between active and passive roles and the sadomasochistic violence that produces them also inform Mizer's *Jealous Cowboys* made a year later. Unlike *Nevada Smith Posing*, *Jealous Cowboys* was not a posing film, but a short narrative. In that film, from a hidden place aligned with the camera's look, we watch a drama between two cowboys unfold. The film's title appears over a picture of a mountain range and, like *Nevada Smith Posing*, this film also attempts to evoke the Western through minimal effort. The precursory set-up involves the arrival of a cowboy who accuses another man of cheating with his wife, indicated by the framed picture of a woman that he is holding. The punishment for adultery meted out by the cowboy involves the accused first being threatened by a gun, then forced to strip naked, tied to a bed, and further threatened with castration by an open razor held near his penis. On paper this sounds rather sick but it is unconvincingly performed and clearly engineered to provide a maximum quota of male nudity. The threat of violence and castration is a way of providing motivation for a striptease and close-up shots of the penis. In a reversal of fortune the accosted cowboy grabs the other's gun and turns the tables. Now forcing him to strip, he also gets naked, but instead of threatening him with castration he forces himself upon the other cowboy and begins to kiss him. The cowboy says to the other 'what the hell are we fighting over a chick for?' before telling him to 'turn her picture around'. The framed photo is placed face downward on the table and thus the woman's look is averted and she is denied any position to see within this exclusively homosexual scenario. This also relates to the logic of the Western in which the woman represents the curtailment of the cowboy's freedom and the potential to disband his all-male kinships. Here she is dispensed with in what one assumes to be the real rather than pretend desires of these cowboys.

Violence in *Jealous Cowboys* functions to legitimate close contact between male bodies that otherwise would not take place. The linkage between violence and homoeroticism, evident also in the other Westerns discussed and wholly characteristic of Bob Mizer's oeuvre, especially in wrestling films, draws to the surface the Western's repressed sexualities and desires that find themselves recoded and experienced as violence. Warhol knew it and it would seem that Mizer did too. In *Brokeback Mountain* violence is often Ennis's response to his desires and feelings. The first sexual encounter in *Brokeback Mountain* appears to take on the aura of violence as Ennis wrestles Jack into position on all fours. Ennis's feelings of shame after sex come to be symbolised in the sheep he finds violently torn apart the next day, and when Aguirre spies on Jack and Ennis through his binoculars he catches them wrestling. Just before they leave Brokeback for the first time, instead of a kiss, Jack and Ennis begin fighting. The only way they are able to deal with the departure seems to be through physical violence which brings them into close contact one last time. The blood resulting from this fight is left stained on the two cowboy shirts that Jack, then Ennis covet so dearly. The violent contact of their first departure becomes a tender memory stained in the checked fabric.

Conclusion

The first section of this chapter examined *Brokeback Mountain* in relation to the Western genre by demonstrating how the film reworks the dialectic of wilderness versus civilisation. *Brokeback Mountain* is a queering of the Western because it purposely places homosexuality in the midst of formulaic oppositional structures and queers them through contact with concepts important in queer theory including homophobia, the closet, silence and heteronormativity. The Western as a cultural form opens up a forum for debate, questioning the role of wilderness and civilisation in relation to sexuality, revealing how gender and genre might correspond and regulate one another, highlighting the production of the closet in rural contexts, and telling the story of two homosexual men who cannot negotiate a gay identity. In doing so, *Brokeback Mountain* draws out a particular site of repression that also concerns a wider veiling of homosexuality in the genre and its mythology.

   In the second section I diverged somewhat from analysing *Brokeback Mountain* more directly with the intent of doing some of this unveiling. *Brokeback Mountain* provokes us to explore some of these broader relations concerning Westerns and homosexuality and in turn enables a better contextualisation for the film itself within a loosely defined history of what we might provisionally call the 'queer Western'. This, as I have already suggested, was not meant to be an overarching history but, rather, a selection of queer moments in the production and reception of several Westerns that have proved particularly fascinating. I looked at six different films as a way of showing how similar themes and ideas have existed throughout the genre's history from classical studio Westerns to underground independent movies, and contemporary remakes. The point of this selective history is to reveal how the Western has always been, to varying degrees, in contact with homosexual and queer themes and issues. Sometimes these are latent but at other times they are resolutely manifest. All the different production contexts seem to highlight, whether covertly or explicitly, a homoerotic fascination for the cowboy, and the slippages between the homosocial and the homosexual that seem germane to the genre. In the course of this material, I am convinced that throughout the Western's history, the genre has functioned to repress, sublimate and manage homosexuality as its foundation has been steeped in an obsession with images of men, masculine rituals and male friendships. This makes the unexpected popularity of *Brokeback Mountain* all the more important because the indie film shatters convention in suggesting that the Western can no longer keep its queer history closeted.

3. A Pathetic State of Affairs: *Brokeback Mountain* and Melodrama

Introduction

The preceding chapter positioned *Brokeback Mountain* in relation to the Western genre. Yet, despite the plethora of ways in which this relationship was explored, the ensuing analysis did little to explain how *Brokeback Mountain* was affecting and emotionally involving. The obvious affects of the film are the production of a feeling of powerlessness and pathos and of a heightened emotional response to what is a perspicuous topic for gay and lesbian audiences, the destructive forces of the closet and rural homophobia. The consequence of all this is tears. The power of melodrama to produce intense feelings has often constructed it in direct opposition to the stoic affects of the Western as a more serious genre of masculine agency. There is an obvious attempt to see these genres as separate through their imagined and assumptive social function and the gendering of audiences. In this chapter I will explore the melodramatic form and affects of *Brokeback Mountain* as a queer melodrama that promotes negative feelings and explain why feeling bad is important for queers and how melodrama is the mode through which *Brokeback Mountain* achieves this.

Passionately Passive

Emotionally wrought and brimming with pathos, *Brokeback Mountain* perhaps did not appear to be explicitly political in its solicitation of emotion. This is because in soliciting overly emotional responses and attachments, especially crying, passivity and over-identification with separation and loss, the film (any film) leads one quickly to the assumption that such affects, which are both passively and passionately experienced, tend to evacuate all seriousness, reason and propriety. This line of thought, which has been particularly pertinent to feminism, helps set up one of the themes of this chapter, passivity. As Sara Ahmed explains:

> It is significant that the word 'passion' and the word 'passive' share the same root in the Latin word for 'suffering' (*passio*). To be passive is to be enacted upon, as a negation that is already felt as suffering. The fear of passivity is tied to the fear of emotionality, in which weakness is defined in terms of a tendency to be shaped by others. Softness is narrated as proneness to injury. The association between passion and passivity is instructive. It works as a reminder of how 'emotion' has been viewed as 'beneath' the faculties of thought and reason. To be emotional is to have one's judgment affected: it is to be reactive rather than active, dependent rather than autonomous.[1]

In surrendering ourselves to the power of films like *Brokeback Mountain*, which makes us cry and lose control, we are assumed to renege on reason and seriousness, and to circumvent political efficacy. If this is true, then is it possible for a film so deeply attached to provoking passive and excessive emotional states, especially feelings that are depressive and negative, to become the source of progressive politics? I would argue that, indeed, the film can produce a multitude of political gains as besides belonging firmly to the generic category of the Western, *Brokeback Mountain* is also a prime example of a melodrama, which in many ways counteracts the restrained affects of the Western. The film's melodramatic mode and form that are masterfully constructed through narrative situations of separation and loss, and suffering and failure, its temporal organisations of knowledge and its discrepancies in point of view between character and spectator cannot but produce feelings of helplessness and pathos. Furthermore, *Brokeback Mountain*'s stress on negative and depressive histories of the homosexual past help to constitute contemporary gay and lesbian identity and subjectivity as, according to Heather Love, 'the experience of queer historical subjects is not a safe distance from contemporary experience; rather, their social marginality and abjection mirror our own'.[2] Importantly, melodrama as a cultural form is about the refusal of distance, favouring instead closeness and an over-identification with those who are hard done by. Exploring *Brokeback Mountain* as a melodrama requires one to touch upon theories of melodrama as developed in film studies but also, and necessarily, queer theory, which has permeated my approach to the Western genre in the previous chapter. In this chapter I would like to examine queer theory's recent turn to a politics that embraces negative feeling. As I will argue, where *Brokeback Mountain* triumphs is in the way these two critical concepts, melodrama and queer negative feeling, dovetail with one another to produce an affective and emotionally queer film experience that is epistemological, temporal, passive, helpless, negative and pathetic.

Melodrama: Genre and Backwardness

Melodrama is a flexible category with a history of shifting meanings that often challenges generic essentialism in film and thwarts efforts towards a neat categorisation of filmic texts of that designation. Like *film noir*, melodrama is sometimes considered a mode rather than a genre proper, although I would suggest it is more constructive to approach melodrama as a consequence of that particular tension between genre and mode. As a term originally derived from French theatre in the eighteenth century, melodrama (etymologically a combination of the Greek words *melos* (song) and *drama* (to play or perform)), can be applicable to such a broad range of texts as to sometimes appear meaningless; unless, that is, one makes a clear case for historical contextualisation and cultural specificity. For instance, the melodramatic stage plays in eighteenth-century France dramatised the struggle between the aristocracy and the middle classes around the time of the French revolution. Political tensions were configured through the conflicts of characters clearly portrayed as either good or evil. In melodrama proper there was no middle ground. This polarity between good and evil was organised through costume, gesture and music, and was represented in strongly iconic terms as representational excess. As Peter Brooks explains, the monarchy and the church were weakened during that period of French history and could no longer provide a moral order for society. A new moral order had to be reinstated and melodrama became the cultural form that sought to realise this change of guards.[3]

Melodrama clearly defines what is good and bad by using certain conventions of form which are evident in a range of media, from music and print media to the reality television sob story with its by now well-known convention of narrating tragedy with a particular use of music that evokes pity. The important point to glean from the historical origins of melodrama is that, as a cultural form, melodrama was seen as a way of perceiving the world in response to specific social pressures. Therefore, one can propose that *Brokeback Mountain* as a melodramatic form of film is importantly placed to utilise the genre or mode in order to narrate to great affect the ongoing problems of the closet and homophobia in contemporary gay and lesbian social, cultural and political life.

In the context of cinema, melodrama can refer to a range of films and periods, including: the early cinema of sensational serial drama and the perilous films typified by D. W. Griffith's dramatic rescue films; the woman's film of classical Hollywood with its themes of maternal sacrifice and family conflict exemplified by films such as *Now, Voyager* (Rapper, 1942) and *Mildred Pierce* (Curtiz, 1945) in the 1940s and a number of films by Douglas Sirk in the 1950s (*All that Heaven Allows*, 1955 and *Written on the Wind*, 1956); contemporary weepies like *Love Story* (Hiller, 1970) and *Steel Magnolias* (Ross, 1989) with their rollercoaster of emotions; popular European 'art films' such as those associated with Rainer Werner Fassbinder and Pedro Almodóvar; independent films of the 1980s such as the AIDS dramas *Parting Glances* (Sherwood, 1986) and *Longtime Companion* (Rene, 1990) and more recent indie films such as *Brokeback Mountain, Far From Heaven*, and *Savage Grace* (Kalin, 2007).[4]

Despite the broad range of often seemingly unrelated films that can be termed melodramatic, there is a small number of formal devices and narrative structures that are often evident in the majority of films of that designation and which are also central to *Brokeback Mountain*'s definition as a melodrama. These include: an expressive use of music (the *melos* of melodrama) to produce heightened emotions; discrepancies in point of view that create complex hierarchies of knowledge;[5] and the timing of narrative events that are mobilised to induce tears.[6] While dealing with all these structures of melodrama is beyond the scope of this chapter, I would point the reader to Chapter 4 of this book and the extended discussion of one stereotypical melodramatic scenario: the scene in which Alma witnesses Jack and Ennis's kiss in the stairway nook, which is an example where a shift in the hierarchy of knowledge, our momentary alignment with Alma as she discovers Jack and Ennis kissing, produces an anxious discrepancy between character and spectator's point of view. The role of music in *Brokeback Mountain* is also discussed later.

Brokeback Mountain has been positioned within the melodrama debate by Jim Kitses and Ara Osterweil, both writing in a *Film Quarterly* special issue on the film.[7] Osterweil views *Brokeback Mountain*'s relationship to melodrama as conservative, especially in regard to the film's resolution, and she describes how melodrama 'ultimately contains the radicalism of its subject matter through generic conservatism'.[8] I would disagree with any claims to conservatism vis-à-vis *Brokeback Mountain*'s particular queering of melodrama. Following inspiration from Heather Love's work on historical injury and contemporary queer identity, it would seem that one can also propose that melodrama is also an important form that can deal with queer experience.[9] In her book *Feeling Backward*, Love explains why hurtful, melancholic and depressing experiences also constitute contemporary queer identity and thus need to be acknowledged, incorporated and negotiated since 'many of these unlikely feelings are closely tied to the realities of queer experience past and present'.[10] In this respect, *Brokeback Mountain* is a text that has a backward logic. It uses the past to speak to the present as it narrates a depressing story of historical injury and bad feeling in order to connect to a contemporary audience who may feel that they are still negotiating or finding it difficult to dispel a shameful and homophobic past – homosexuality is problematic! Love continues:

Backwardness means many things here; shyness, ambivalence, failure, melancholia, loneliness, regression, victimhood, heartbreak, antimodernism, immaturity, self-hatred, despair, shame. I describe backwardness both as queer historical structure of feeling and as a model for queer historiography.[11]

Many of the terms in Love's above quote may describe the characters and their narrative situations as well as the spectator's response to the film. It is important that the film does provoke negative and bad feeling. It is not a joyous experience; rather it is a film that leaves one feeling hurt and emotionally devastated in its backward turn. Yet, this is somehow what is rewarding about the film. It is *Brokeback Mountain*'s melodramatic form that allows it to express and evince a history of injury, backward feeling and affectivity through the conventions of melodrama that work so well in dealing with themes and structures of secrecy, pathos, passivity, paranoia, shame and temporal irreversibility.

In more general terms, Linda Williams has considered melodrama a 'backward-looking form' that does not always move towards the future while Christine Gledhill has suggested that 'melodrama frequently stems from such an attachment to an outmoded past'.[12] It would therefore seem that melodrama and queer historical injury are bound to one another as they deal with the past and negate a happy future for the characters, while forcing the spectator to confront an excess of bad feelings. Melodrama is a form that appears to be ideal in its potential to explore and confer on the spectator an emotional and affecting experience that allows the painful history of queer life to be connected to the present. In other words, Jack and Ennis's history is a more broadly conceived queer history. Melodrama is one such genre or mode in which this historical and contemporary interconnectedness can be culturally and aesthetically articulated. If anything, melodrama is an emotive cultural form and a tactical way of provoking feeling and sentiment that are politically efficacious.

Music and Emotion

There is no melodrama without music. Music is a central component of melodrama and is 'the privileged signifier of affect' as it is for cinema more generally.[13] The film's score often tells the spectator how to feel or how to respond to a scene. Music supplements the narrative and image. Music is part of the package of overall affect that melodrama produces, which reaches its zenith when the swelling of upward movement and increasing loudness in the score equates to a rise in emotional feeling and the welling of tears. One can feel emotion stirring both in the mind and through the body as if the music were itself teasing it forth. The intensity of sound always seems to match the intensity of affect so that a certain dissolution of the two is possible. As Thomas Elsaesser put it:

Music in melodrama, for example, as a device among others to dramatise a given narrative, is subjective, programmatic. But because it is also a form of punctuation in the above sense, it is both functional (that is, of structural significance) and thematic (that is, belonging to the expressive content) because used to formulate certain moods – sorrow, violence, dread, suspense, happiness.[14]

Before its critical revaluation in the 1970s, the expressive use of music in classical Hollywood melodrama was no doubt part of the reason for its dismissal as the music was often overwrought and omnipresent. The exaggerated and highly expressive music, Romantic in its use of strings, colludes with notions of the genre's inherent manipulation of emotions as both effeminate and excessive or lacking in restraint.

Music of course plays a very important role in *Brokeback Mountain* and one must mention composer Gustavo Santaolalla's victory at the 78th Academy Awards, a victory that attests to the music score's quality and credibility. However, quality and credibility do not necessarily suggest that the music was restrained and lacking in excessive intent. In addition to the score which is non-diegetic, *Brokeback Mountain* is also represented by diegetic incidental music which is often heard on the radio (for example in Jack's truck) or as live music in the social spaces represented in the film. The role of diegetic music in the film, predominantly of the 'country and western' genre, is cultural in the sense that it brings credibility and verisimilitude to the eras and the people. The function of non-diegetic music in *Brokeback Mountain*, the Santaolalla score, is expressive rather than cultural. The score belongs to the sphere of melodrama, whereas the country and western music does not.

An important scene in *Brokeback Mountain* with respect to *melos* is the closing shots of the film in which we share a final moment with Ennis alone in his trailer. His daughter has just visited but has left her jumper behind. Ennis is about to put it away in his closet and as he begins folding it the closet door is opened and we see both Jack and Ennis's cowboy shirts from their time as young cowboys. The shirts are hanging together on the inside of the closet door below a postcard depicting Brokeback Mountain. Throughout these moments the music begins, with the familiar chords of the guitar that resonate with memories of the film utilised one more time to signal the end of the film. Unofficially this piece of music is Jack and Ennis's theme although the track is called 'The Wings'. Ennis buttons up the shirts together and in the following shot we see a close-up of Ennis's face with tears in his eyes as he says 'Jack I swear'. Ennis closes the closet door, moves out of shot and the music gets louder, the shot remains for several seconds before fading to black and the credit 'Directed by Ang Lee' appears.

Revisiting this scene for the purposes of analysis is itself traumatic and it is the music that contributes a great deal to the sort of anguish that I have been characterising, following Heather Love, as backward feeling. The description of this scene fails to capture its pathos and power. The music allows for emotions to tip over and become overwhelming through the way the score functions as a memorialisation of their togetherness and their eventual loss. The music serves as a leitmotif for Jack and Ennis and its final occurrence at the end of the film marks this as a memory. It is important that the music here also accompanies the image of Ennis's closet and the two shirts contained therein. The affectivity of the music necessarily underscores the important theme of the closet and repression's tragic consequences. The music allows for the freedom that the closet restrains and thus functions as a form of release that the narrative itself cannot confer. The melodramatic affect of the music here is one that emphasises the closet as destructive force, symbolising Ennis's well of loneliness, at the same time as it allows a sort of relief by provoking cathartic tears in the spectator. The music cues emotion and provides an outlet for the spectator in relation to the repression and pent-up feeling that the narrative can never properly resolve because of Ennis's conflicted sexuality and the fact that in melodrama it is always too late.[15] Music provides an amplification of the emotional registers of the narrative but it also provides the spectator with an outlet for the hopelessness and melancholy that we share in our empathy for Ennis.

As an aside, 'The Wings' is the only piece of music from *Brokeback Mountain* to have an interesting afterlife. It appeared on gay dance floors on both sides of the Atlantic. 'The Wings' as an unofficial theme was predominantly remixed as a beat driven and percussion heavy house track, specifically tribal house. The remixes involve filtering effects and a breakdown in the middle section, a beatless section that remains close to preserving the original form of the track as heard in the film, which structurally emphasises in this moment the emotional resonance of the music in ways that clearly invoke the pathos of identifying with Ennis's loss and backward feeling. There are a number of issues that I think are important here in terms of music, melodrama, and the score's queer afterlife. The affective quality of this particular piece of music continues to remind queers of the pain that was and still is often part of queer life. Even the contemporary experience of ecstatic abandon in dance music culture cannot dispense with the melancholia of queer history. The freedom to dance ushered in by disco is not representative of a broader sense of freedom since homophobia is still out there beyond the safety of the club. Hearing *Brokeback Mountain* in the disco is perhaps a reminder of this and a nod to the fact that a broader understanding of melodrama as a cultural force may in fact constitute a way of negotiating queer life more generally.

'Feeling Homosexual': Pathos and Passivity

Passivity, pathos and also pathetic and passionate are a cluster of terms which orbit around the melodrama and also share a similar semantic field and etymological roots in both Greek and Latin. I am drawing attention to this overlap in meaning because an argument can be made that brings together affects associated with pathos and feeling pathetic with the suggestion that melodramatic pleasure generates emotional and corporeal passive experiences. *Brokeback Mountain* is steeped in pathos as the feelings of pity and compassion that we feel in relation to the film's characters and their situations, and which we can do nothing about, are the consequences of melodramatic form.

The original meaning of the word *pathos* in Greek denotes suffering and sensation and also provides the root for the adjective *pathetikos*, which in Greek means sensitive, but which in the English language has produced the word pathetic, which has different connotations. That which is pathetic, like pathos, has the ability to produce affective and moving responses when it is mobilised as a quality of art. To feel pathetic is to let something affect us as we become recipients of outside stimuli, allowing ourselves to be entered by feelings. Similarly, to be touched by something also suggests an emotional touch as well as a touch that conveys some sense of materiality in that the body is touched. Passive experiences are often materially registered through the body (for example, holding your hands up to your face, looking down and refusing eye contact and crying, all physical responses that denote a deference or loss of control).

However, if we remain for a moment with the Greek account of the term pathetic (*pathetikos*) we find that it has another meaning which has a good deal to say about the relationship between queerness and affect in *Brokeback Mountain*. To say in Greek that a man is pathetic is also to say that he is homosexual and to strictly delineate between an active and passive sexual role. The term active is opposed to the term pathetic rather than passive, as it is in English. The question of whether one is active or pathetic is tantamount to the question of whether one is straight (or acting straight) or gay, if he 'gives it' like a man or 'takes it' like a woman. The coding of the terms and their role are worked through in a logic that views gender as the axis upon which definitions of heterosexual and homosexual masculinities become perceived as either active or passive/pathetic, to do or to be done by.

Feeling pathetic is thus related to queer feeling; debasement, melancholy and emotional surrender have currency in *Brokeback Mountain* as Love's explanation of backward feeling suggests. As a particularly queer experience of melodrama *Brokeback Mountain* renders passive experience in political terms because it unsettles cultural assumptions in the relationship between gender, spectatorship and genre. Passivity and male homosexuality have often aligned as ideal defining characteristics of 'the homosexual'. This particular essentialist association is a production of knowledge in the invention of homosexuality, a way of on the one hand explaining homosexuality as a trope of gender inversion and on the hand, following Foucault, a way of connecting particular acts to particular identities.[16] This inversion discourse secures the essence of hegemonic masculinity as an active agent who does not 'get done to' what he 'does' to others. My intention in this section is to champion the kind of passive pleasures provoked by melodramatic forms of culture such as *Brokeback Mountain* as an important way of contextualising emotional experiences within a distinctly queer framework.

The man who willingly gives over to the pleasure of passive sensation flies in the face of hegemonic masculinity's propriety to secure its separation from the Other which is commonly identified as the effeminacy of woman. The role of the discourse of inversion or the woman trapped in the man's body (vice versa for lesbians) seeks to explain how homosexual sex and the homosexual are often reducible to a feminised receptivity. However, gay male culture has its own gender-phobic language of separation (bitch, queen, Mary, Jessie, etc.) in which effeminate or sexually passive gay men are devalued in relation to those gay men who appear to be closer to the ideals of hegemonic forms of masculinity (the so called 'straight-acting' ones) precisely because the queens are apparently closer in their relationship to women and femininity. Certain aspects of this culture are indefensible as misogyny as Richard Dyer has convincingly argued.[17]

To re-orientate the debate back to cinema, cultural resistance and even the labelling of some classical Hollywood films as 'the woman's film' signify these films' apparent threat to male spectators (the imagined hegemonic kind of spectator at least) who might be affected by melodramas in ways that promote enjoyable passive pleasures such as crying and pathos, which are culturally constructed and understood as feminine. Part of my own pleasure in melodrama, supported by the status of melodrama and female stardom in gay *cinephilia*, is the way the genre compels one to let go and surrender to feelings of pathos, sadness and helplessness, as well as to over-identify with suffering protagonists, frequently female ones. This, I would argue, is one way in which melodrama could be seen as a pathetic form of 'feeling homosexual' but in a way that also challenges the stigmas attached to passivity and reception so often devalued and debased as effeminate and sentimental, which in turn fosters suggestions that they lack critical perspicuity and should not be taken seriously.

On the widely circulated film poster Jack and Ennis and their tilted heads and downcast eyes seem to eschew the confrontational look and stoic posturing of men in cinema (and especially in Western films) and in doing so appeal to a sorrowful and pathetic mode of masculine performance, a performance of backwardness perhaps. Ennis is a pathetic spectacle and his performance works hard to secure such meanings. Another way of reading this would of course be to characterise the image as one of shame. Even before the film's release in the theatres, the poster already invokes the pathos it will provide if you are willing to take it. As I argued in the previous chapter, *Brokeback Mountain* is a text that is both a queer variant of a genre and a queering of genre itself and this applies to its status as a melodrama too. As a matter of fact, one particularly queer element of the film is the way it irks the distinctions between the categories of the Western and the melodrama as frequently gendered genres.

The powerlessness, the constant waiting and the emotional vulnerability that melodramatic structures of storytelling induce create an experience of passivity and helplessness. Mary Ann Doane describes the pathetic text as one built on a series of disproportionate relations 'between means and ends, desires and their fulfilment'.[18] It is these disproportionate relations that produce pathos and passive experience. In *Brokeback Mountain* 'the very mechanism of pathos' is Jack and Ennis's persistent efforts to be together only to be constantly hindered by obstacles, the greatest of which turns out to be Jack's death.[19] The distance between Ennis and Jack and what they are trying to achieve is marked by numerous instances of disproportion: they live at a significant distance from each other; Ennis cannot resolve his homosexuality in the way that perhaps Jack does; they are separated by class; Ennis is often torn between his role as a father and his need to live up to heteronormative ideals which constantly conflict with his desire and role as Jack's lover and partner.

The last point illustrates clearly the mechanism of pathos in the scene where Jack goes to meet Ennis on the same weekend the latter has arranged to spend time with his children. After receiving a message from Ennis that his divorce has come through, Jack races up to his farmhouse. We see Jack in his truck with a smile on his face that signals the potential for fulfilment. When Jack arrives, however, he is confronted by Ennis and his two daughters, and the happiness that one might expect to see in Ennis following the news of his divorce from Alma is quickly quashed by his excuses and mumbling. The children become a means to avoid dealing with his repression and his paranoia since Ennis keeps his eyes focused on a passing car in the distance. Typical of the melodrama is this quick shift in emotional register from a moment of happiness to one of pathos. The scale of disproportion is often realised in the extreme states of emotional polarisation when joy turns to sadness and the protagonists find themselves once more in contradictory positions. Jack leaves in his truck, with the hope of them being together quickly dissipating, and heads towards the Mexican border where he pays for a hustler. Jack's unhappy departures in his truck are a recurring motif in *Brokeback Mountain*, a repetitive situation that underscores the stasis in their relationship and the pathos in themes of deferred and unfulfilled desire. As Doane explains:

In this sense the pathetic text appears to insist that the gap between desire and its object is not structural but accidental and therefore to reconfirm the possibility of fullness in signification – a complete and transparent communication. Tears testify to the loss of such fullness but also to its existence as a (forever receding) ideal.[20]

It is significant that when Jack departs in his truck on both occasions (the first departure after they first meet and the second in this later scene) the shot inside his truck spends a considerable amount of time on his crying as he comes to terms with the endless deferrals. This is yet again an example of the melodramatic device in which a discrepancy in knowledge between character and spectator operates to produce anxiety and helplessness in the spectator. Ennis is not aware of how Jack really feels and we are the only witnesses to Jack's disillusionment and turmoil. Pathos is produced because we cannot do anything to let Ennis know what we know.

A good deal of the pleasure of *Brokeback Mountain* is about 'letting go' and allowing oneself to be emotionally overcome by the devastation caused by closetedness and repressed desire as we wait for Jack and Ennis to get together, which of course never happens. *Brokeback Mountain*, like the woman's film of the 1940s analysed by Doane, emphasises a constant waiting: waiting for Jack and Ennis to get together; waiting to see how they will respond in particular narrative occasions; waiting to see what will happen next with the hope that it is joyful rather than tragic. This foregrounds 'waiting' as a particular manifestation of passive desires.[21] Melodramas, especially in their alternative categorisation as weepies and tearjerkers, have been associated with emotional duress and unfulfilled resolutions concordant with waiting, female spectatorship and female pleasure. This is because it is commonly assumed that women are naturally constituted to take pleasure from a passive surrender to their feelings, of which delay and tears are two such consequences, a theme perhaps crystallised by Jack's tearful moments in the truck.

Both historical and contemporary accounts of homosexual men have often sought to render their sexuality meaningful through the way in which homosexuality, like femininity, is constituted by a wilful passivity. The most obvious translation of this idea is the assumption that gay men are the ready recipients of anal sex and like women they are defined as the ones who 'take it' willingly. As a matter of fact, in many cultures and situations homosexuality is often defined as the willingness to occupy the passive role, the pathetic position, often leaving the top role, the active inserter, to remain free of the pathological stigma attached to homosexuality because this role is not one that connotes debasement and surrender of masculine power. This logic skews sexuality through rigid and heteronormative conceptions of gender in which real men remain active and women and homosexuals are constituted by passivity. This also recalls the argument presented in Chapter 2 which explored Eve Kosofsky Sedgwick's thesis in *Epistemology of the Closet*, and specifically that the distinctions between heterosexuality and homosexuality are made meaningful through other sets of binary opposition such as active and passive.[22] Gay and lesbian studies and queer theory, as well as feminism before them, have frequently sought to understand the role that passivity occupies for the concepts of gender and sexuality. Therefore, it is worth commenting on how the passivity and thus the pleasures of melodrama generated by *Brokeback Mountain* are significant for a queer politics.

Writing at the height of the AIDS crisis in the 1980s, Leo Bersani advanced an argument that saw the fear around gay men's receptive sex practices as engendering a radical alternative to social and moral policing around concepts of self and society.[23] Bersani characterises the pleasures of receptive sex as self-shattering as it undoes the self through an abdication of mastery, power and control and 'the tyranny of the self'.[24] The gay man's 'legs up in the air, unable to refuse the suicidal ecstasy of being a woman' is a pleasure that is based on a refusal, negativity and a loss of control.[25] It is this unimaginable desire of being fucked (erroneously what some people think defines male homosexuality) that seems to go against the psychic, corporeal and social coherence of men, masculinity and the male body normatively conceived of in terms of the one who does things to others, both masterful and controlling, in its most extreme form equating penetration with domination. Because the self is shattered so is its relationship to a concept of male community and male relations.

Paternal melodramas like *Written on the Wind* are also like Bersani's account of anal sex. Although this sounds like a bizarre analogy, on a closer look they both deal with a sensational and ineffable power that tends to the breakdown of a patriarchally defined masculine self, male relations and community. Building upon Bersani, Judith Halberstam collects together a number of queer scholars' writings under the rubric of an 'anti-social turn in queer studies' that is 'anti-communitarian, self-shattering and identitarian'.[26] Halberstam also proposes a useful phrase in 'radical passivity' as the 'refusal quite simply to be', suggesting a way in which letting go and being overcome with emotion and pathos are characteristics of a radical position worth adopting.[27] Watching *Brokeback Mountain* does not really make one feel that subjectivity and self are being undone, but those tremulous feelings of not being able to hold back the tears and of feeling helpless as we watch Jack and Ennis grow more distant, or when Ennis breaks down and holds on to Jack, and any scene in which they separate from one another, does make losing control and pathos feel somewhat pleasurable.

The fact that such negative feelings can be pleasurable is certainly a queer aspect of *Brokeback Mountain* as melodrama since it goes against propriety and common sense attached to what it means to be a man. Men who are aroused by passivity, whether sexually or in the case of *Brokeback Mountain* emotionally, ebb at hegemonic masculinities. This also signals a challenge to the gendered coding of film genres and their essentialised concepts of the audience that has often attempted to separate the Western from the melodrama. Geoffrey Nowell Smith explains this as follows:

Broadly speaking, in the American movie the active hero becomes the protagonist of the Western, the passive or impotent hero or heroine becomes the protagonist of what has come to be known as melodrama. The contrast active/passive is, inevitably, traversed by another contrast, that between masculine and feminine.[28]

That genres can be related to active and passive experiences foregrounds the arbitrary way in which cinema is regulated according to an essentialising notion of gendered form and experience. Theoretically speaking, an issue with *Brokeback Mountain*'s status as a Western might be that it offers a passive experience of an active genre that, as ludicrous and unconvincing as it sounds, is something akin to experiencing a man's genre as a woman. The conflicted nature of gender in this context is that *Brokeback Mountain* disallows generically gendered separations as an aspect of its queer undoing. The Western is thus non-normatively experienced in *Brokeback Mountain* through the passive and pathos-driven pleasures commonly associated with melodrama and the woman's film.

Conclusion

In adopting a melodramatic mode through which to tell its story *Brokeback Mountain* perhaps gestures towards the fact that homosexuality is still a difficult and emotive subject. The backward feeling and the pathos articulate a refusal to see progress in the way it is often imagined. *Brokeback Mountain* demands that we accept that homosexuality is still impossible for many, that it is still permeated by tragedy and melancholia, and that it has a history that is still unresolved and needful of being properly negotiated in the present. The fact that melodrama provokes bad feelings is a politically affective response and those negative feelings need to be considered as politically efficacious. This was explained by situating theories and concepts of melodrama alongside queer theory, in particular Heather Love's concept of feeling backward. *Brokeback Mountain*'s melodramatic mode helps remind queers that their modern subjectivity is constituted by a painful, closeted, homophobic past and that 'feeling bad' is an important affective dimension of queer subjectivity in the present. Passivity and pathos were also particular consequences of *Brokeback Mountain*'s melodramatic conventions and structures. Pathos is a central component in melodrama and the origin of the word in Greek also brings with it a history of meaning that refers to homosexual men as pathetic. This collapse in meaning between pathos and pathetic was a way of suggesting how the passive pleasures of melodrama might also be considered queer. Therefore, 'feeling bad' and 'feeling pathetic', the politicisation of emotion and affect and the disproportionate relations between past and present are what make *Brokeback Mountain* meaningful as a queer melodrama.

4. When Jack and Ennis Meet: Cruising as a Mode of Gay Spectatorship

Introduction

This chapter considers a sequence of shots in *Brokeback Mountain* and their relationship to gay spectatorship. More specifically, it is concerned with interrelationships between gay male cruising, spectatorship, and editing that in combination overlap much more than one would expect. The argument I will be developing here is based around one shot/reverse shot sequence comprising only six shots, lasting forty-three seconds in total. This sequence would seem to invite an interpretation of film form that conflates cruising and editing as one mode of gay spectatorship. The staging of a cruising scene at the beginning of *Brokeback Mountain* helps to establish a specific reading of some of the film's editing patterns, in particular shot/reverse shot in which two men's looks collude, through a lens of gay spectatorship and gay cultural knowledge. This initial cruising scene also informs the interpretation of several subsequent instances of shot/reverse shot in the film.

The interpretation of the scene when Jack and Ennis first meet also contributes to a more general concern related to shot/reverse shot editing and how gay spectatorship might challenge any neat alignment of shots whose logic is understood as heteronormative. What I mean by this is that there is an obvious male–female complementary logic that is privileged in the interpretation of film form through an antithetical understanding of gender difference. This stems from theories of spectatorship, especially those that follow on from Mulvey's feminist intervention.[1] While offering a valuable and much needed criticism of cinema as a patriarchal institution, Mulvey's argument is heteronormative because it is unilateral in its structuring of desire and power through the concepts of the male gaze and female to-be-looked-at-ness. Lee Edelman refers to this canonical position as an assumptive 'determining relation of sexual and visual logics'.[2]

Difference in the cinema is defined through gender often conceived of as a unilateral power play but it is also heterosexual in terms that are necessarily vexed from a gay and lesbian perspective. I will argue *contra* that cruising as a particular structure of gay male looking relations closely resembles the same formal structures of cinema that have assumed a gendered frame rather than one that accounts for queer sexuality. It is my aim to establish and corroborate specific relations of looking and glancing between men that are bilateral and decidedly different from the unilateral gazing of much film theory. *Brokeback Mountain* employs in its construction of homosexual desire a shot/reverse shot structure that makes available a reading of film form based on a same-sex logic rather than the gendered difference that otherwise characterises 'straight' readings and framings. In doing so, I will briefly sketch out the history of shot/reverse shot and the attendant theories of spectatorship that have made sense of the editing pattern. Furthermore, I will demonstrate that the subjective counter-shots that establish as a structural motif the cruising and subsequent desire of Jack and Ennis are inverted in two point of view shots that threaten to expose, from an objective position external to the couple, their secret unity. These latter 'closeting shots', Joe Aguirre's and Alma del Mar's point of view shots, emanate from an outside position that I will characterise as working to produce the closet and counter the allegiances and emotional investments that are nurtured in gay spectatorial modes of viewing *Brokeback Mountain*.

The Subject of Gay Spectatorship

The concept of the film spectator is a thorny issue in film studies and now so inherently problematic that it always comes packaged with provisos and caveats. It may even be worth avoiding it altogether for the trouble it might get a scholar in. This is because the film spectator is an abstract idea, a theoretical concept, and an effect of the text as opposed to a real viewer in an actual lived relationship with the cinema. One also has to be careful not to merge the spectator with other similar terms like 'audience' and 'viewer' that are synonymous in everyday speech but particular and differentiated in academic discourse. Contemporary film studies see the spectator of the 1970s as a shameful embarrassment of the past. The concept is a bad object and the language through which it came into being is now seen as prejudicial through the way it allowed the construction of a particular universalised and ahistorical subject of the cinema. The prevailing idea was that the spectator is a subject position who is a consequence of the text's formal organisation and institutional arrangement of technology. Spectatorship was an ideological position that is furnished for us through an erasure of how image and sound is put together and an effacement of the conditions in which the film is projected on the screen in the darkened theatre.

After the spectator, the 1980s introduced us to the film audience and the film viewer, a real living constituent of moviegoers who had a cultural identity that they brought to the cinema. Audiences and viewers could be observed and quizzed for their attitudes to film and their histories of moviegoing. The shift from spectator to audience accounted for cinema as historically determined and archive-able, international in scope, identity-defining in relation to pleasure, and an object of popular culture. This stood in contradistinction to the mid-seventies psychoanalytic moment characterised by the import of Althusser, Freud and Lacan in seminal articles by Jean-Louis Baudry, Christian Metz, and of course Laura Mulvey.[3] The concept of the audience instead drew on traditions from cultural studies and anthropology, examining participation and negotiation as active components in the meaning-making of the cinema experience. In this context it was the other way around, not the spectator as an effect but the text and the institution as effects of the audience; an audience with an agency and cultural identity that exists in a historically determined point in time. A simplified account of this polarity would have at one end the spectator, for whom meaning is created by film form and the conditions of projection, while at the other end would be the viewer, a real person, who creates meaning actively.

This spectator/viewer schism is a dilemma that has not only distinguished between different periods of disciplinary inquiry but also different methodological camps, traditions and theoretical allegiances. The difference between the spectator of film theory and the audience of cultural studies is not monolithic since both disciplines arrive at their conclusion about the cinema from differing intellectual histories. Judith Mayne has cleared the most workable path through the thicket of real and imagined incompatibilities between spectatorship and viewership, between subjects and real people, film theory and cultural studies, when she asks us to consider spectatorship as 'precisely those spaces where "subject" and "viewers" rub against each other'.[4] It is now a given that the spectator is problematic but this should not rule out the potential for the concept in an adaptive and nuanced form to still explain in part how we are both affected and affecting in our relationship to the cinema. Mayne goes on to suggest that film studies 'attests to a discomfort' in its relationship to the spectator it created 'with either a too easy separation *or* a too easy collapse of the subject and the viewer'.[5]

Even though the subject of spectatorship in film theory is, as Mayne argues, not always a real person, gay spectatorship as a concept, as I will argue, in part relies on a gay person for it to even be theorisable. In this respect, I do acknowledge that theories of spectatorship are so vexed that it makes it difficult to proffer any kind of claim that gestures towards the subjectivity and identification of apparently real viewers – for example a gay moviegoer – that in some way is not always already contestable. Whatever one proposes to say about spectatorship and the spectator is already set up for a hostile response through the thorny 'discomfort' that Mayne characterises as a disciplinary symptom. The concept of the gay spectator that I wish to develop here is one that is produced out of the rub between spectator and viewer. It is a hybrid between spectatorship and viewership or reception. My account of gay spectatorship is what nestles in the middle of the schism, affecting and being affected. In the queerest way it cuts across and transverses, not remaining in allegiance with any one side.

Therefore, gay spectatorship is made meaningful in this context as both a passive effect, for example, how we are positioned to see in relation to editing, and an active one, effecting through the knowledge, identity, experience and historical context that a gay man brings to the viewing of a film. This does not mean that gay spectatorship is an exclusively furnished position for the gay male moviegoer, nor specific or intrinsic to all gay men. Rather it is the closest alignment between the situation I aim to describe in *Brokeback Mountain* and the cultural identity most close to decoding it. Surely, one could argue, a film that is about male homosexuality, same-sex desire and the closet should be addressing the gay spectator, whomever I imagine him to be, who should be in a privileged position to most readily recognise a film about him. However, I would not argue that my experience of the text and how I made sense of it was a correlative of other gay men's receptions and experiences of *Brokeback Mountain*. While the text can produce the same position for us all, gay or straight, since its form is limited to how the text has been constructed from a series of shots, it does not necessarily mean that my identity or anyone else's relates to these structures in the same way and that all spectators can see specific moments in *Brokeback Mountain* as being akin to cruising. I am arguing here that the knowledge and social experience of gayness affects the potential interpretations that can be drawn from the text and at the same time the text in return, at the very least, can stimulate such readings through specific formal arrangements.

The way I am using the concept of the gay spectator here is open to phobic reactions against its obvious essentialism. However, such a situation has a necessary get-out-clause thanks to Spivak's notion of strategic essentialism.[6] Strategic essentialism ascertains that at certain times essentialism is necessary to marginalised people in order for them to be recognised as a group and act politically. The cost of championing the gay spectator is to a certain degree essentialist, though far from an absolute. Thus I am willing to go along with it here as a necessary political gain if the argument I present is to be of any value in contributing to debates about spectatorship and the agency of a gay subject of the cinema.

This is also why the concept of queer spectatorship as an anti-essentialist manoeuvre is not always a preferable term because sometimes it is vital to inhabit the context of gay and lesbian studies rather than the dismantling protocols of queer theory. Queer theory may in fact de-gay the very specificities that are required if the gay spectator is to be meaningful and viable as a category of analysis in spectatorship. To argue for the political efficacy and gains of the gay spectator, essentialism is a risk worth taking. Although this does not mean that the concept of the gay spectator is uncritical or unproblematic, it is not tautological either. Here strategic essentialism functions in its capacity to be a temporary strategy that can establish a specific set of viewing relations in a category of viewer called the gay male spectator. The strategic aspect of the endeavour is being employed in a specific way to define a set of viewing relations that straddles a real gay viewer and an imagined position that draws upon analogies between the culture of cruising and film form. Strategic essentialism also brings with it knowledge of the dangers of essentialism itself, though any wilful agreement with or contestation of this proposition will at least contribute in some way to furthering the concept of gay spectatorship, whether essentialist or not. Any counter claim can only seek to further clarify the concept of the gay spectator.

The topic of gay men and lesbians and their relationship to cinema has been an important one in film studies since the British Film Institute's publication of Richard Dyer's *Gays and Film* in 1977.[7] Recurring features in the theorisation of gay men and lesbians' relationship to the cinema involve questions of investment, fascination and obsession with, more often than not, Hollywood cinema and stars.[8] The gay spectator in this instance is constructed almost exclusively through his reception practices that may include sharing a passion for cinema with other gay men, identifications with stars, and camp viewing strategies.[9] The most sustained account of the gay spectator, in relation to what might be called the passion-for-cinema-position, is to be found in Brett Farmer's *Spectacular Passions*. For Farmer, whose argument is far more complex and compelling than I am allowing for here, the gay spectator is defined through receptions (of Hollywood genres), negotiations (camp strategies), and identifications (with the maternal) that characterise a special set of relations between gay men and the cinema.

Farmer invites us to rethink more broadly a theory of fantasy and cinephilia as complex determinants in a gay spectatorship at once both social and psychic. There are overlaps in Farmer's concept of the gay spectator and my own in that we are both concerned with reading relations and gay men's agency, pinpointing what gay men bring to and also take from cinema, both socially and psychically, in order to negotiate their position as hyphenate spectators-viewers. My own argument is a lengthy addendum to Farmer, and when I mention the gay spectator it implies the work already covered in *Spectacular Passions* even as I detour from his central concerns with psychoanalysis and fantasy. Furthermore, the concept of the gay spectator here is not an overarching sweep to define all gay spectatorships; rather it is a specific attempt to account for the momentary overlap between cruising and editing.

The Cruising Scene in *Brokeback Mountain*

After the Focus Features logo *Brokeback Mountain* begins with a series of establishing shots of the landscape accompanied by a terse plucking of the guitar. Wyoming 1963 appears on screen and as night turns to day we see a truck dropping Ennis Del Mar in the small town of Signal. Ennis leans against a cabin, waiting hopefully for his summer employment from Joe Aguirre, and soon after a small beaten up truck draws in beside the cabin. In a long shot we see Jack Twist get out of his truck on the far right of the frame while on the far left of the frame Ennis leans against the cabin. Jack Twist kicks his truck and then slowly turns around to face Ennis who appears to be ignoring Jack's arrival. What follows in this opening scene is a forty-three second sequence of six alternating shots structured as shot/reverse shot in which Jack and Ennis both return looks and glances at each other. A table describing each shot and an illustration of them are produced below.

Shot number and length	Type of shot	Description of shot
Shot 1 10 seconds	Long shot	Jack Twist getting out of his truck and slowly turning around and facing the direction of Ennis del Mar. Jack poses with his hands on his hips and looks directly at Ennis.
Shot 2 5 seconds	Medium long shot	Jack's point of view shot is a medium long shot of Ennis del Mar leaning against the cabin. Ennis avoids looking out from under his hat but we infer he knows Jack is looking at him.
Shot 3 8 seconds	Close-up	Jack is looking directly at Ennis with his head slightly tilted. Jack looks down and then turns away so that Ennis can look without being seen to be looking.
Shot 4 5 seconds	Close-up	A close-up shot of Ennis pretending to look straight on (not in Jack's direction) but he furtively looks to the right and steals a glance at Jack.
Shot 5 12 seconds	Medium long shot	A medium long shot of Jack who turns around and returns Ennis's look while leaning back against the truck in an aloof pose. Jack fixes his look on Ennis before tilting his head down.
Shot 6 3 seconds	Extreme close-up	An extreme close-up of Ennis sitting down reflected in the wing mirror of Jack's truck. We can hear Jack rinse his razor, thus we infer that he is using the mirror. This is confirmed in the next shot.

The shot/reverse shot pattern in this sequence might appear conventional at first. The most basic function of this pattern is narrative realism through spatial continuity that both establishes the relative position of two bodies in space and fixes the spectator in relation to their fictive looks. It can, therefore, as a matter of fact be treated as a simple continuity structure: the shot/reverse shot pattern is one of the most frequent continuity devices in cinema, most recognisable during conversation scenes. In shot one we see Jack looking and in the second shot (the counter-shot) we see what he is looking at, in this case Ennis. Similarly shot four repeats this by establishing that Ennis is returning

Figure 6 Shot 1 (© Focus Features)

Figure 7 Shot 2 (© Focus Features)

Figure 8 Shot 3 (© Focus Features)

Figure 9 Shot 4 (© Focus Features)

Figure 10 Shot 5 (© Focus Features)

Figure 11 Shot 6 (© Focus Features)

the look. Shot/reverse shot often establishes the look of the character by having the first shot of the character looking followed by the second shot of what he or she is looking at; this is commonly supported through an eye-line match.[10] The function of shot/reverse shot is primarily to construct coherent spatial relations between shots so that we know how one shot, as a representation of narrative space, corresponds to a preceding or subsequent shot. It often tells us who is looking and what they are looking at. Thus we can argue that the function of shot/reverse shot is to create contiguous spaces in temporal simultaneity out of a sequence of shots. The spectator infers that the sequence of shots are connected spaces, and therefore a relationship between two shots and two spaces, or two people, is created through the arrangement of shots in a formal system.

What I am proposing here is that some instances of shot/reverse shot are not just simply continuity patterns, or for that matter reducible to heteronormative gaze relations. The shot/reverse shot pattern described above bears some kind of relation, however arbitrary, to the cultural practice of gay male cruising. Certain shot/reverse shot sequences between two men appeal to the gay spectator by being recognisable as such. In *When Men Meet*, Henning Bech's account of cruising also reads like a description of this scene.

You look away *almost* as soon as his eyes hit yours; and after a moment, you look back to see if he's looking at you. Now it's his turn to shift his eyes; this must happen quickly, in any case, and the very speed of it – i.e. whether the pace is a little slower or a little faster – will map out the likelihood of further developments.[11]

The exchange of glances and gazes across the six shots, the looking and the not looking, work as an alternating sequence of shots. In this sequence, it is not simply to recognise cruising as taking place *within* a single shot, as in a two-shot in which two men eye each other up, but as a structure *between* shots in a play of looks that goes back and forth as one shot responds to another; one shot looks back at the other, and so on. Bech also describes cruising as 'a combination of gazes and movements' and one can translate this 'combination' in terms of 'the gaze' being firstly, represented by the single shot of Jack and his point of view shot and secondly, 'the movement' as multiple shots through editing and the shot/reverse shot pattern between both Jack *and* Ennis who looks back.[12] The point I want to stress clearly is to differentiate between what happens in a single shot, as a narrative image, when one looks and what happens between multiple shots, as a formal pattern, when both looks are stitched in a process of exchange. In *Brokeback Mountain* the initial shot/reverse shot pattern that situates Jack and Ennis in a spatial relation to one another is one that I will argue closely reproduces a structure of cruising. An analysis of shot/reverse shot patterns in *Brokeback Mountain* speaks to both an imaginary position for gay spectatorship and the potential for recognition among gay viewers of a scene of cruising in the cinema. Furthermore, the manner in which the shot to shot relations (which often include the point of view shot) work as a formal device also corresponds to debates and questions in theories of spectatorship such as the notorious concept of suture. A number of these debates emerged once again in the 1970s, when the subject of spectatorship came to fruition. I will attempt to reinvigorate some of these debates here as a necessary means through which to qualify the concept of gay spectatorship in relation to editing.

Cinematic Cruising and Shot/Reverse Shot

The emergence of editing and shot/reverse shot, sometimes called angle/reverse angle cutting, was not a feature of primitive cinema, and was not developed until 1907. Eileen Bowser dates the beginning of editing, then called 'alternate scenes', as occurring in the transformation period between 1907 and 1908.[13] She describes alternate scenes as 'the development of new ways to connect shots' that gain prominence during the period of transformation. This is the beginning of editing as a system that involves cutting to connect different shots in order to create more narratively complex spatiotemporal worlds, what Bowser refers to as 'a kind of geography made of separate shots related to one another'.[14] Bowser also goes on to explain how the introduction of editing integrated 'the spectator more deeply in the film experience' and how alternating scenes 'would greatly increase the potential for enlisting the spectator's emotions', which suggests the establishment of a closer relationship between affect and form.[15] In *The Classical Hollywood Cinema* Kristin Thompson explains that shot/reverse shot in particular becomes an occasional practice increasingly evident in the years between 1911 and 1914.[16] Thompson also points out that shot/reverse shot structures begin to appear in films 'where a two-shot could easily have been used' therefore, the decision of the director to cut the scene into different shots is considered a new alternative to the previous convention of using one shot featuring two people.[17] By 1915 the shot/reverse shot structure shows signs of becoming a standard practice. Barry Salt confirms this as a 'definitive development', ushering in the continuity system of editing that defines the classical Hollywood paradigm.[18] An interesting point in this early cinema history is that shot/reverse shot becomes an alternative to the two-shot prior to the introduction of sound and the conversation scene. This does suggest that the relationships between characters as two separate shots are meaningfully connected through formal relations in editing rather than sound and dialogue.

There are close associations here with the opening of *Brokeback Mountain* that unfolds in a dialogue free silence. We do not need a verbal exchange when shot/reverse shot can tell us about Jack and Ennis's interest in one another. As a gay spectator I have already recognised that their interest in one another is that of desire. The six shots are also complementary, with three shots of each character that structure an exchange based on a same-sex logic that is equal rather than a gender disparity that is unequal and unilateral. The logic of cinematic looking that emerges in theories of spectatorship following Mulvey, which needs no rehearsal here, assumes a male subject who is looking and in the counter-shot a woman being looked at.[19] In the shot/reverse shot structure between Jack and Ennis the looking and who is being looked at are based on a bilateral exchange, a same-sex logic that neither favours one individual as the subject nor the other as the object; although one could argue that Jack's look is the more assertive one and therefore is afforded a longer shot duration. This scene translates the structure of same-sex cruising into cinema since the practice of cruising depends on a reciprocity and recognition of each other's looks that the unilateral male–female looking relations of classical narrative cinema rarely seem or want to accommodate.

Descriptions of gay male cruising often stress the reciprocity of the glance and the often playful exchange of looks. Bech suggests that the homosexual gaze is a look that often lingers, it has that extra beat of time, which is more obvious in Jack's shots which last longer at ten, eight and twelve seconds. Again, Bech's description of cruising sounds like this scene from the film.

Here it is a matter of seduction. So the gaze must be audacious, it must linger – not too long, but longer than otherwise, then be taken away again slightly slower than otherwise, as if sticking voluptuously to the other's and only reluctantly tearing itself away from the toffee.[20]

Ennis's look is less direct, more stolen; like Bech's concealed glance he is the one who likes to see without being seen. Ennis's shots only last for a few seconds. Cruising can also be fleeting and ephemeral. It can take place when two gay men pass each other on the street or elsewhere. Ben Gove cites artist David Wojnarowicz who described cruising as 'extended seconds'.[21] The duration of each shot also confirms this with the shots of Ennis's concealed glance, that Jack allows in his deliberate turning away from him; these are brief but significant 'extended seconds'. Jack's more confident looks (he after all initiates the cruise in the first shot) are twice as long as Ennis's. Gove emphasises the temporal nature of the cruiser's glance when he describes cruising as 'a sense of time expanding during the exchange of erotic eye signals, as the two gazing men create a circuit of desire that arouses the circular, self regarding timelessness of the unconscious'.[22] There is a knowing acknowledgement of each other in those fleeting glances and the all-important return look that confirms the interest of each party. Ennis steals a look every time Jack seems to turn away. Jack of course turns away because he wants Ennis to look without being caught in the act. The six shots in *Brokeback Mountain* only constitute a fraction of the film but they are extended not just in their duration but also in terms of extending their importance for a position that would seem to appeal to the gay spectator.

The outcome of cruising is not always sex – this sequence of shots attests to that – as cruising might simply be a confirmation of reciprocal interest or mutual acknowledgment of one's homosexuality. Cruising is often too neatly collapsed into metropolitan promiscuity that often suggests that it is more of an urban manhunt than a series of meaningful glances and gazes. The account of cruising I will contend with here is one that places emphasis on structures of looking rather than sex and promiscuity and it can take place beyond the urban sprawl. It is an acknowledgement of the interest and desire of seeing and being seen as the logic of exchange.

Cruising is explored in a range of gay cultural forms and it has a rather elevated status as an intrinsic feature of urban gay male culture where it is often mythologised in discourses of self-discovery, sexual abandon, and tutelage. In the 1970s learning how to cruise, to read another man's look as a gesture of mutual interest, was also bound to a notion of learning to be gay itself and the *sine qua non* of the pick-up. In 1981 the gay disco act Boys Town Gang sang about cruising over a disco beat in their thirteen-minute opus 'Cruisin' the Streets'. Included among the lyrics is a long list of real cruising hotspots in several US cities. Cruising has been a recurring feature in gay literature from coming out fiction to pulp erotica and it commonly features in art and photography ranging from Paul Cadmus and Tom of Finland to Steven Klein's homoerotic photo shoots in *L'uomo vogue*. The 1978 liberation era publication *The Joy of Gay Sex* included cruising in its alphabetical listing of sexual practices where they describe it in the following way:

> There is an art to cruising, and its most important tools are timing and the eyes. The eyes first: You're walking down the street and you pass a man going in the opposite direction. Your eyes lock but you keep on moving. After a few paces you glance back and see that he has stopped in front of a store window, but is looking directly at you. [. . .] After a bit, the frequency and intensity of exchanged glances will increase, and one of you will stroll over to the other.[23]

Again, the emphasis on temporality, reciprocity and the glancing exchange is echoed in the cruising scene in *Brokeback Mountain*.

Cruising and the cinema are also related in another way. From the beginning of cinema, film theatres were often meeting places for clandestine affairs and public sex between men. In his history of queer London, Matt Houlbrook indexes no fewer than twenty West End venues by name in which men used to meet other men for sex in the dark and in front of the screen.[24] Since its inception the cinema has been central to the cultural and sexual life of gay men in which the darkened venues hosted all manner of insouciances and cruising activities. In an unintentional humorous nod to early cinema, Houlbrook recounts how the Biograph cinema near Victoria Station was nicknamed the Biogrope due to the amount of cruising activity taking place.[25] While this kind of activity petered out in most cinemas due to increased public knowledge concerning the sexual activities of men of questionable reputation, cruising found its niche in adult cinemas showing heterosexual porn. Heterosexual porn was merely a smokescreen for closeted and uncloseted men to meet in safety for anonymous sex. The French film *Le chatte à deux têtes* (Jacques Nolot, 2002), also known internationally as *Porn Theatre* or *Glowing Eyes*, takes this situation as its very topic in exploring the dissolutive effects on the fixity of sexual identity in a Parisian porn theatre. In Tsai Ming-Liang's *Goodbye Dragon Inn* (2003, Taiwan), the screening of a martial arts film before the closure of a cinema affords a Japanese tourist one last opportunity to go cruising.

Cruising and film spectatorship have been explored twice before and they have also been linked to channel surfing in queer television.[26] I would like to summarise the two arguments pertaining to film in order to confirm the relationships between cruising and spectatorship but also incorporate my own argument about how cruising and/as spectatorship can be theorised.

R. Bruce Brasell examines a scene of cruising in Warhol's *My Hustler* (1965) in order to suggest more generally how cruising, as a glancing look rather than a gazing look, might be a more productive theorisation of how gay men are positioned to see in cinema. For Brasell, the gay spectator's position relates to cruising because his look at the screen and his look in the film are often characterised as glances. The cruising-derived glance is posited as a more useful definition of looking for gay spectatorship because it also challenges the 'hegemony of the gaze as a metaphor for describing spectatorship'.[27] Brasell is right to assume that the gaze is permeated by a monolithic status in theories of spectatorship which, as I suggested earlier, is heteronormatively conceived. He also considers the look of the gay spectator in the cinema's auditorium whose 'glance implies that the screen may not always be a safe place for the spectator, that the spectator may be forced emotionally to look away, an experience common to gay men'.[28] This argument suggests that gay spectatorship is in a direct relationship with the cinema screen, a relationship that often asks the gay spectator to only look fleetingly at the screen, to furtively glance rather than remain fixed in a penetrating gaze. Brasell's theory of gay spectatorship as cruising is one in which the spectator is in a process of exchange with the screen itself.

My Hustler is an unusual choice from which to explore this proposition since the film only contains two reels with static camera set-up. My own reading of *My Hustler* is that it does not contain any obvious cruising per se between the characters. The spectator never participates because there is no editing and what is at first assumed to be a point of view shot of Paul America on the Fire Island beach, because we hear an off screen discussion about what we are seeing, in fact turns out to be a subjectless pan from Warhol's anonymous camera. Warhol's cinema is one of voyeurism rather than cruising. In the second reel of *My Hustler*, Brasell does claim that the bathroom scene when identified through gay subcultural knowledge is 'a cruise in the disguise of a banal discussion about hustling'.[29] What is evident in his interpretation of *My Hustler* is an allegory in the glance for gay spectatorship itself. The film's second reel, which takes place in front of a mirror in which the glance comes to be mediated through reflection, resembles the shot of Ennis in Jack's wing mirror. The look in *My Hustler* is neither direct nor fixed but materialises from somewhere else, a reflection. This 'other' place is the social margin that gay men, including Warhol, often occupy and is translated through the screen's organisation of looking relations. The two important points that Brasell's theory of gay spectatorship proposes are his introduction of the cruiser's glance as an alternative to the gaze and his emphasis on the subcultural knowledge of cruising that the gay spectator brings to the cinema.

The glance is also a feature of Nicholas de Villiers's article on gay spectatorship in which he introduces cruising as one of his queer ways of looking. The glance remains a clandestine, stolen and furtive look that often characterises and implies the gay man in films like *Advise and Consent* (Preminger, 1962) and *Far From Heaven*. De Villiers comes closer to my own account of gay spectatorship and/as cruising in his perceptive analysis of *Death in Venice* (Visconti, 1971) in which he reveals how the spectator becomes *implicated* in the cruise between the ephebic Tadzio (Björn Andrésen) and the ageing Aschenbach (Dirk Bogarde).

The camera's movements in each of the scenes in fact attest to a double effect of visibility. When Aschenbach first sees Tadzio in the hotel lounge with his family, the camera alternates between panning around the room, finally 'landing' on Tadzio, and close-up shots of each ('reaction shots' of Aschenbach to Tadzio's beauty). But this panning is not actually a point-of-view shot, rather, as it pans 'back' from Tadzio, the camera includes Aschenbach in the frame. This technique is repeated throughout the film in elaborately choreographed camera movements and zooms, thus acting as a lesson in cruising – framing and constructing Tadzio as beautiful 'to-be-looked-at object,' and making Aschenbach's desire visible – and rendering Aschenbach himself visible as potential spectacle.[30]

The emphasis on camera movement and spectacle function to implicate the spectator in the cruise and identify the desirable object of the cruise as Tadzio. However, in de Villiers's account we are watching the cruise unfold from a position beyond the exchange of the looks that is otherwise between two men onscreen and often in long take, rather than through cutting. Tadzio is never afforded a point of view shot in his looking back. Our look is never his look, thus we are cut out of any bilateral exchange. In this particular scene of cruising our look as spectators also comes from outside the text as it is filtered through the camera's anonymity. In theories of spectatorship this is the distinction drawn between primary identification, in which we see events unfolding but are not part of them, and secondary identification in which the look of the camera merges with the look of the character and we see from a position within the fiction.[31] We observe the cruise in *Death in Venice* but often from the objective position of narration that hinders our participation in the cruise on a formal level. This is significantly different from what takes place in *Brokeback Mountain*.

The representation of cruising in the cinema is not the exclusive domain of gay men. There are other examples including that brief queer moment in *Calamity Jane* (David Butler, 1963) when the eponymous heroine first arrives in Chicago and bumps into a woman on the street who turns, winks and smiles. In Brian De Palma's *Dressed to Kill* (1980) one central set-piece is a ten-minute long sequence in an art gallery in which Angie Dickinson's interest in art is merely a ruse to pick up a stranger for anonymous sex. Of course her appropriation of a gay cultural practice paradoxically gets her hacked to death by a queer psychopath. Heterosexual pick-ups on the street and clandestine anonymity also flavour Patrice Chéreau's hardcore art film *Intimacy* (2001).

Jack and Ennis look at each other in nearly all of the six shots and, as I have been stressing, the cruising takes place not just in the shot as an image but also in the relation of shots as editing. Cruising can be displaced on to the text as the relationship between one shot and another, that is, shot/reverse shot is structured somewhat like cruising. The relation of shots is an act of confirmation that the look of one shot is recognised in another. Therefore, and unlike the other examples of cruising in the cinema, it is editing as well as narrative and camera movement that constructs cinematic cruising as a mode of gay spectatorship. In this sense we not only recognise the scene of cruising as observable narrative information, as de Villiers does with *Death in Venice*, but we actually participate in the cruising on a different level through editing. There are countless scenes of gay male cruising in the cinema which we can readily identify, but in the *Brokeback Mountain* sequence we are not only witnessing the cruise between Jack and Ennis but also stitched in through the shot/reverse shot structure. Cruising in this instance is about editing as much as it is about looking and the particularities of shot/reverse shot work to stitch us into the exchange in the closest way possible to an actual cruise – if that were possible! The particular choice of vocabulary ('stitched in') here is deliberate. It invokes the concept of suture and the way in which what at first appears as an objective shot becomes in the next a subjective one. A discussion of suture will help explain how cruising and spectatorship relate to one another through a chain of shots.

Suture

Suture remains a fairly notorious concept in film studies, testament to the obtuse and near impenetrable direction that film theory was taking in the 1970s. Suture is a concept that many have heard of but rarely pay any attention to since its introduction in film studies.[32] I will admit that my first encounter with the suture dossier in *Screen* over a decade ago was an experience of befuddled incomprehension and frustration. I am not alone in this response because the original text's lack of transparency required a lengthy exposition by Stephen Heath, reworking the theory into a tangible concept for film scholars. Suture was symbolic of everything that was wrong with 1970s film theory's universalising claims and incomprehensible abstractions.

My explanation and use of the term here is more of a suture-*lite*, less tautological and totalising, and certainly less psychoanalytic than its original incarnation as proposed in Jacques-Alain Miller and Jean-Pierre Oudart's writings.[33] I am emphasising the role of suture in further explaining how gay spectatorship can relate to specific instances of shot/reverse shot because suture usefully explains how shots relate to one another in order to produce meaning for the spectator. Stephen Heath has called suture a 'position of exchange' which is an expression that also sits comfortably alongside cruising as that other system of exchange.[34] Cruising in the cinema and the system of suture closely relate to shot/reverse shot patterns in order to inscribe point of view in narrative space. However, Heath cautions against a view that only reduces suture to shot/reverse shot. In the sequence from *Brokeback Mountain* suturing is the process through which we get stitched into Jack and Ennis's exchanges and understand how this positioning can be understood as a cinematic form of cruising.

Suture is a term that originally derives from medical jargon where it means to stitch the lips of a wound or of a cut together. Suturing closes a gap. In film theory, suture also closes a gap, one opened up by an encroaching awareness of off-screen space, but this all takes place as an unconscious activity and in psychoanalytic terms relates to 'the junction of the symbolic and the imaginary'.[35] Suture's theoretical basis depends on this stitching or closing of an unconscious anxiety-inducing gap that threatens the subject's coherence in the symbolic.[36] In cinema, the spectator's experience of film also comes with a potential rupture that there is nothing that exists beyond the frame and outside the shot. Daniel Dayan relates this idea to a classical painting in which there is nothing that exists beyond the edge of the canvas and frame.[37] What is outside is referred to as an absent field inhabited by the look of an absent one or an absent mediator who is not us. It is the empty void of the fourth wall. The absent one is a look we see but from someone perceived to be not there at the same time, an outside mediator who is not a character in the fiction but an enunciating system that draws too much attention to the text as a construction.

The next shot or counter-shot covers over the perception of absence initiated by the first shot by making it appear to be the origin of a look from a character coming from inside the fiction. The second shot responds as if the first shot were coming from the place of absence in the first shot. The second shot is signified by the first shot and the threat of absence that there is nothing beyond the shot is stitched together and closed over by having it originate as a look or point of view coming from within the narrative space. Suture's job is to turn absence into presence, keeping us inside the fiction rather than outside the text. When the former shot is configured by the latter shot it turns the enunciation of narration into the fiction of narrative as the reverse shot enables the spectator to identify the off-screen space as his or her look. The gaps' suturing together for the spectator occurs when the next shot posits an origin for the first shot by inscribing it as the point of view of a character rather than an unknowable and anonymous absence. Absence threatens to reveal the text as nothing more than an arbitrary series of shots. It is suture's task to keep up the illusion of fiction.

Suture is closely related to continuity editing and the shot/reverse shot structure is the model through which the unconscious process seamlessly turns an objective shot into a subjective one. Film editing by its very nature fragments the spectator's look through a constant disruption that shot/reverse shot counters by telling us where the look in the fiction originates. Suture helps to inscribe a point of view that helps to efface what Dayan calls 'the system that speaks the fiction'.[38] The subjective and the objective shots become reciprocal and dependent on one another to construct a comprehensible experience of continuous time and space. Regardless of the unconscious implications, it does appear as if the shots respond to each other's need, much like they were cruising. The shots seem to cruise each other, looking for mutual recognition in their exchange and in turn confirm each other's existence. There is a dependency that stitches together each shot in a potential structure of desire for the other shot. Only when the cruised (of the second shot) returns the look does the cruiser (of the first shot) understand the situation to be such and if no look is returned then no cruising is taking place.

The suggested links between suture and cruising are cannily explained by the dynamics of the shot/reverse shot pattern that they both share. Both cruising and suture depend on giving meaning to the first shot or person that the second shot or person has determined is looking. The return look or second shot is what determines that two shots or two people are related through a system of looking. Only when it becomes the point of view of another look in the second shot does the first shot relate and close the gap opened up by the anxiety of the unconscious over the absence or the 'cruised's' lack of interest. Suture's second shot is characterised by the cruiser's backward glance – the return shot that gives the first one its meaning and origin. Without the stitching together of the two there would be no meaning in shot-to-shot relations or rather no cruising taking place.

If we return to the sequence of shots in *Brokeback Mountain* we can see this taking place. One shot responds to another and so on. In every shot there is an absence but that absence is filled up by the next shot when we occupy the position we imagine to be either Jack or Ennis. In turning those absences into characters, alternating our position as one between seeing and being seen, placing us inside the fiction, we are effectively stitched into the very act of cruising that shot/reverse shot facilitates. My argument here is that shot/reverse shot and suturing turns our absence into a presence and supports a reading of the sequence as cruising by implication. The reverse shots enable the spectator to see as both Jack and Ennis, cruising each other, enabling unspoken desires, and structuring a position as alternatively of the looker and the looked in a context of exchange familiar to many gay men.

The Rhetoric of Shot/Reverse Shot

The principal emphasis in this chapter has been on a single scene when Jack and Ennis meet for the first time. I have suggested this reproduces cruising as a specific mode of spectatorship and that this may be especially resonant for gay spectators. Shot/reverse shot is a standard continuity device in narrative cinema and the coherence of *Brokeback Mountain* frequently depends on the management of temporal and spatial relations that this pattern of editing achieves. There are countless shot/reverse shot structures throughout the film that work invisibly in the service of continuity but there are also several other important shot/reverse shot sequences that require additional comment for the ways they establish connections between film form and sexual politics, and the tensions and concomitant gestures that they produce in relation to spectatorship, gay or otherwise.

During the early campsite sequences there are two significant and very telling shot/reverse shot scenes between Ennis down in the campsite and Jack up in the mountain. In these sequences neither Jack nor Ennis know that they are the objects of the other's point of view shot. They switch jobs at one point and this eventually leads to Ennis staying in the campsite, leading to the first time they have sex. These two shot/reverse shot sequences happen before the tent encounter and inscribe a sense of longing and desire to be together that predicates that first sexual encounter.

Shot/reverse shot marks this out as an inevitable outcome from the cruising scene to these two additional sequences. The second shot in both these two shot/reverse shot structures is marked as a point of view shot and is imbued with a desire to eradicate the spatial gulf that keeps the two men separated by work. These two shot/reverse shot sequences that follow on from the cruise carry with them an emphasis on their relationship through the formal relations of shot-to-shot. The suggestion here is that editing often brings Jack and Ennis together and structures them in a relationship at the formal level even if the narrative and Ennis's reticence often keep them apart.

Every shot/reverse shot in which Jack and Ennis are significantly structured in relation to one another is also a history of their relationship told through form. Those first six shots (the shot in the wing mirror that is repeated again when they depart for the first time) and the shots between the mountain and the campsite are a chronicle of their desire written in shot relations. This idea is confirmed close to the end of the film in an emotional scene when Jack and Ennis are together for the very last time. These last moments are devised through a sequence of temporally dissonant shot/reverse shots and fit well with asynchronous time which has been a hallmark of both queer temporality and melodrama, in this case the alternation between Jack and Ennis of 1963 and 1981.[39]

When Ennis breaks down (the 'I wish I knew how to quit you' scene) in 1981 and Jack comforts him, the shot slowly dissolves into a shot of the campfire, a memory from 1963. We see first in a long shot and then in a close-up an intimate hug (this tender shot is reproduced on the cover of this book) in which Ennis sings a childhood song into Jack's ear before heading up to the mountain. Following this is a sequence of four shots in a shot/reverse shot pattern. We first see in an over the shoulder shot Jack watching Ennis depart on horseback followed by a counter-shot of Jack. Both these shots are from 1963. The next shot is again what Jack is looking at but this time it is Ennis's truck leaving for the last time in 1981 and in a second counter-shot we see Jack looking but being significantly aged. The editing pattern blurs the two timeframes of the film by having 1963 and 1981 collapse into a scene in which Ennis departs and Jack looks on. They also mark the high point and low point in their relationship, which, like many other significant instances, is marked out by a particular use of the shot/reverse shot pattern. These last shots in which they are together take on a tremendous significance as Jack's literal looking back in the editing becomes a figurative looking back at their relationship. The look back is not only the backward glance of the cruiser and the counter-shot of editing, but it is their history of having never been able to be together in the way that one would wish. To borrow Heather Love's term, it is an instance of 'feeling backward' that characterises a queer sense of loss, a pathos-tinged look back at the happiest moment when they were in love (the subject of Chapter 3).[40] If they first met through a concerted use of shot/reverse shot then this is logically how they depart for the last time. Their relationship is bookended by shot/reverse shot and in this scene they are undone by the same kind of editing that brought them together in the first place.

The very last three shots of the film are also haunted by this structure. The third to last shot in the film is a close-up of Ennis's face as tears well up in his eyes and he says 'Jack I swear'. This is followed in the counter-shot by a close-up of what he is looking at: the collars of the two shirts nestled together and the postcard of Brokeback that Jack sent to Ennis in

1967. Jack is dead but his presence is there not just through the shirt and the postcard but through the memory inscribed in form that emphasises how meaningful the shot/reverse shot structure is to the gay spectator's understanding of their relationship. In addition to the emotionally connected objects in the *mise en scène*, the counter-shot of editing is the spectral signifier that reminds us of Jack. These two shots are important for understanding how shot/reverse shot is significant in *Brokeback Mountain* especially if we attempt to construe it as something more than just a simple pattern of continuity.

As a gay spectator I have imagined colluding with Jack and Ennis's cruise and can interpret something both specific and important in the logic of reciprocation, the desiring glance, and the looking back that shot/reverse shot seems to enable. If the gay spectatorial response makes possible the mutual inculcation of shot/reverse shot and cruising then such a position may equally disinvest or refuse to be stitched into other instances of the same pattern, especially those that counter with the potential to tear apart something so carefully sewn together by a secret same-sex desire. As I will demonstrate in the remainder of this chapter, there are two shot/reverse shot sequences analogous to one another which threaten to expose the secret that Jack and Ennis's closet keeps preciously locked away. I am referring here to two point of view shots of other characters, one that is Joe Aguirre's and the other that is Alma del Mar's, both taking Jack and Ennis as their object.

The first shot in the Joe Aguirre sequence is an extreme long shot of Jack and Ennis wrestling and fooling around without their shirts on. This sequence also helps to further explain some of the formal workings of suture. The shot of Jack and Ennis is initially unattributed and thus is characterised as no one's look. This is what would be referred to as either enunciation or narration as it is the look of the camera as mediator; that is, until the next shot when Joe Aguirre comes to take the place of the absent look. This unattributed shot is thus retroactively constructed as emanating from the fiction through our knowledge that it is now the point of view shot of a character. The subsequent shot fills in the gap by ascribing what is off screen to a position occupied by Joe Aguirre whose look is fixating on the men through his binoculars.

The sequence with Alma reproduces a similar logic in that it involves a point of view counter-shot of Jack and Ennis whose secret love is again compromised through someone else's knowledge. The full scene involves Ennis in Riverton waiting for Jack's arrival from Texas after four years of being separated. Jack drives up to the house and Ennis goes down to meet him and they hug. Ennis pushes Jack into the stairwell and begins passionately kissing him as they move out of sight into a hidden nook. The next shot is Alma appearing at the door but staying behind the glass at the top of the stairs. The counter-shot of her look is a high-angled shot from her position that is partially obscured by doorframes and railings (similar to the favoured convention of Douglas Sirk to hinder view through obstacles and props). The objects that obscure the shot emphasise a hidden position of secrecy and surveillance, but also a closeting entrapment or imprisonment that marks the specificity of Alma's look as emanating from an incongruous position that is outside their closet. In the third shot we return to Alma in a close-up of her face registering disbelief as she backs away and closes the door in a symbolic gesture that literally shuts out what she has just witnessed.

Both point of view shots of Jack and Ennis being watched unawares are framed in relation to someone else's knowledge about their sexuality that they otherwise would want to remain a secret. This particular dynamic of surveillance and secrecy in the shot/reverse shot structure is here bound to the production of the closet in which Jack and Ennis's complicity of secrecy allows the potential for another's look to have a certain kind of dangerous leverage. The closet is the destructive force at the centre of the film and these looks are loaded with the threat of disclosure and the confirmation of Ennis's crippling paranoia. It is an outsider's vantage point that is filtered in Aguirre's point of view through the binoculars and in Alma's point of view in the high-angled, obscured look through the window and wooden stair banister. D. A. Miller also links these two looks which take place through glass to the sixth shot in the cruising scene where Ennis is also 'vitrified' in Jack's wing mirror.[41] Miller characterises the vitrification of the image of Ennis as the homosexual observed, one who remains in these shots at a distance, as being seen through glass. This, he argues, produces an optical 'comfort zone' for the spectator who suffers no consequence in being implicated in 'the murderous gaze of the homophobe' and 'the wounded look of the woman'.[42]

Miller is interested in how these shots produce an outside place of viewing for the liberal spectator. I am similarly interested in how individual shots also work to produce a position of spectatorship on the outside but interpret this differently from Miller. Although I see through Aguirre's and Alma's eyes in the literal point of view shot that the function of shot/reverse shot stresses, I do not align myself with their figurative point of view because it comes from a place that also threatens the coherence of gay spectatorship that defines my mode of viewing. I refuse to take up the position of rupture and disclosure, an alignment that I characterise as being incongruous and certainly on the outside, although not in the same sense of outside that defines suture. This outside is wilfully connected to a position that has historically been central to the production of the closet. Miller even suggests that Aguirre's binocular point of view is a murderous homophobic gaze. It is certainly a look of hate and disgust that is confirmed in a later scene through the veiled 'dare not speak its name' expression of 'stemming the rose'.

I also resist sympathising with Alma's position because, firstly, she has the privilege of heterosexuality (probably her only luxury) and secondly, her point of view shot is Aguirre's double in that they render homosexuality with a vitrified and vilified objectivity. In the film theatre when Alma's point of view shot was seen it solicited a sort of 'oh no' gasp on several occasions, which I presumptively interpreted to be the willingness of other spectators to empathetically take up her position; it is also difficult for Ang Lee to resist such a tried and tested melodramatic device as this. Their gasps only strengthen my resolve not to occupy Alma's place, even if her point of view shot forces me to do so. I am also reminded that one interpretation of *Brokeback Mountain* is that it is the story of men who cheat on their wives which I think is exacerbated by the way in which Alma comes to possess the secret.[43]

The question of being outside or dis-identifying, an incongruous positioning and a refusal to take on board the look of a character, even if their point of view shot tries to force us to take it, recalls Nick Browne's important article from 1975 on spectatorship and point of view.[44] In 'The spectator-in-the-text: the rhetoric of *Stagecoach*' Browne questions the authority bestowed on the point of view shot in cinema as one that is assumed to be a coherently prescribed position or placement adopted by the spectator. The fixity of the point of view shot literalises the look of the character and the spectator as one and the same thing. It is a monolithic look that we presume to have no choice in because it is force-fully inscribed in the particularity of point of view's formal design as the definitively subjective look.

In a sequence from *Stagecoach* (John Ford, 1939) Browne distinguishes between two types of point of view which he calls the literal and the figurative point of view. In *Stagecoach* the spectator emotionally identifies with the figurative point of view of Dallas (Claire Trevor) even when the film favours Lucy's (Louise Platt) agency through a stress on her gaze through the literal point of view shot. For Browne the rhetorical aspect of the spectator-in-the-text relates to this tension between the literal and the figurative position of the spectator, a relation to who does and does not have the authority of point of view. In Alma's scene of 'discovery' her literal point of view shot may not always correspond to the figurative point of view which is the emotional connection to Jack and Ennis. Therefore, while we are formally aligned with Alma's point of view we can also exist in a position of dis-alignment to it. My allegiance and emotional investment in Jack and Ennis's relationship fosters my own refusal to allow the collapsing of Alma's literal point of view into any kind of figurative point of view that empathises with her position. Point of view may coincide when the literal and figurative point of view are the same but they may also conflict when the literal makes uncomfortable or comes into conflict with the figurative as my response to this scene suggests. This goes a long way to explaining those moments of gay spectatorship that foster particular modes of identification and pleasure or its opposite. There is always the potential for a discrepancy to open up between the formal, narrative and emotional positions that we choose to take up in relation to how film is mediated as a cultural experience.

Conclusion

The aim of this chapter was to suggest that the scene in which Jack and Ennis meet for the first time may strike a chord of recognition with the gay spectator because it is readily identified as cruising. This was my immediate understanding of the scene upon first viewing, that these men want each other, long before even considering how it was formally constructed. The analysis was also an attempt to contribute to an expanded definition of the gay spectator as he relates to film form, in this instance, editing and point of view. This opening scene also privileges the knowledge of the gay spectator as a cultural viewer in identifying the silent codes of exchange between two homosexual men. In this respect, this is not simply a scene of spatial continuity and I argue instead that editing confirms the gay spectator's position in relation to the film, and the men's relationship, through its structural analogy with cruising. The sequence of shots alternating between Jack and Ennis reproduce a similar if not identical structure of looking and exchange familiar from the cruising scenario and this anticipates further romantic and sexual developments in the narrative. Shot/reverse shot becomes an important system of exchange with a history that stitches together Jack, Ennis and the gay spectator.

As a formal system, editing is different from narrative yet it contributes to the overall meanings generated by the film in terms of how shot relations position us to see narrative events and understand Jack and Ennis's relationship. This is most evident in how their desire for one another and the history of their relationship is in part told through shot relations rather than dialogue. As a gay spectator, my relationship to Jack and Ennis is forged through shot relations as well as the melodramatic solicitations in narrative, sound and performance. This investment and connection to Jack and Ennis is threatened twice by another character's point of view in the film in which they possess the secret of the closeted relationship. I experience an active resistance to aligning myself with another's point of view even though I am forced to see through their eyes. This signals my agency as a gay spectator since I am not always in concordance with the positions given to me through form. A more appropriate concept here would be the hyphenate gay spectator-viewer: a combination that acknowledges the power of cinema but includes the agency of the viewer. My investment in Jack and Ennis, readily implicating myself in their cruise, and the disinvestments in another's look, often harmful, is how film form characterises my spectatorial experience of *Brokeback Mountain*.

Notes

Introduction

1 On emotion and gay and lesbian history see Nealon, 2001; Anne Cvetkovich, 2003.
2 B. Ruby Rich, 2005, 'Hello cowboy', *The Guardian*, http://www.guardian.co.uk/film/2005/sep/23/3 (accessed 9 January 2006).
3 See Tzioumakis, 2009b; Tzioumakis, 2009a, pp. 23–6.
4 The figure was taken from the Internet Movie Database: http://www.imdb.com/title/tt0388795/business (accessed 13 October 2009).
5 Benshoff, 2008.

Chapter 1

1 These definitions are often re-worded from Focus Features' own description of itself from the company's website: www.focusfeatures.com (accessed 23 July 2008).
2 Crothers Dilley, 2007, p. 12. Lee's *Hulk* is obviously considered to be an absolute misnomer in the comic book blockbuster since the film was remade only five years later as *The Incredible Hulk* (Louis Leterrier, 2008).
3 Tzioumakis, 2006, pp. 3 and 9.
4 Tzioumakis, 2006, p. 11.
5 Dilley, 2007, p. 9.
6 Vachon, 2006, pp. 60–1.
7 The figure for the global box office of *The Wedding Banquet* was obtained from the Internet Movie Database: http://www.imdb.com/title/tt0107156/business (accessed 18 Oct 2009).
8 USA Films also produced and distributed a number of films for the home entertainment market.

 9 Lyons, 2000.
10 Lyons, 2000.
11 The data for this table and the rest of the tables in this chapter were collated from a number of sources including the Internet Movie Database, the companies' websites and a number of articles from the trade press.
12 Albert, 2000, p. 14.
13 Harris, 2000, p. 28.
14 Lyons, 2000.
15 Schamus quoted in Rooney, 2004a, p. 30.
16 Studio Canal was the production, development and acquisitions arm of French production and distribution company Canal Plus. Canal Plus is now owned by Vivendi who distributes Canal Plus's vast media library, which also includes the Carolco, DeLaurentis, Embassy and EMI back catalogue, through Universal DVD.
17 Universal Focus was a specialty arm created in June 2000 to distribute foreign films and niche titles in the USA.
18 Lyons, 2002, p. 6.
19 The company's mission statement is available on its website: http://www.filminfocus.com/about (accessed 23 July 2008).
20 Snyder, 2007, p. 49.
21 Schamus, 1998, p. 103.
22 Not to be confused with Lions Gate, which was originally founded by Robert Altman to distribute his own films in the 1970s. Lionsgate Entertainment has gone from strength to strength through its clever exploitation of low-budget horror franchises, having generated a sort of renaissance in extreme gore and torture for the teen market through the *Saw* films (six instalments between 2004 and 2009). Lionsgate is also making inroads through its Lionsgate Television division producing quality series for cable (in the HBO mould) such as *Weeds* (Showtime 2005–), *Mad Men* (AMC 2007–) and *Nurse Jackie* (Showtime 2009–).
23 Vachon, 2006, p. 49.
24 Rooney, 2004c, pp. 8–15
25 See McDonagh, Maitland (2005), 'I've heard that Heather . . .' in *TV Guide* online: http://movies.tvguide.com/movie-news/Ive-heard-Heather-61839.aspx (accessed 19 October 2009).
26 Lyons, 2001, p. 4.
27 McClintock, 2006, p. 1.
28 Wyatt, 1998, pp. 74–90.
29 Dunkley and Bing, 2002, p. 35.

30 Linde quoted in Vachon, 2006, p. 126.
31 Anon, 2003, p. 10.
32 Mohr, Ian (2005) 'Focus unleashes rogue: distrib's mix of edgy and upscale fare will get boost from year-old genre label', *Variety*, 9 May, p. 7.
33 Perren, 2009.
34 Rooney, 2004b, p. 1.
35 Rooney, 2004b, p. 1.
36 Fortado, Lindsay and Dan Hart (2009), 'Universal sells rogue pictures studio to relativity media', Bloomberg, 4 January. Online: http://www.bloomberg.com/apps/news?sid=ai4EstWXFs2c&pid=20601103 (accessed 4 October 2009).
37 Vachon, 2006, p. 230.
38 Rooney, 2004b, p. 1.
39 Kosofsky Sedgwick, 1993, p. 15. In a similar adage, Geoff King refers to the indies as 'the balance of conventional vs. somewhat different' (King, 2009, p. 236).

Chapter 2

1 Kupelian, 2007 (accessed 13 July 2008).
2 Ruby Rich, 2005 (accessed 13 July 2008).
3 Ruby Rich, 2005.
4 Rooney (2004b) refers to the film as 'a cowboy romance', p. 1.
5 Ang Lee quoted in Lang, 2005 (accessed 14 June 2008).
6 Jack Foley quoted in Hernandez, 2005 (accessed 13 February 2007).
7 Proulx, 2005, p. 130.
8 Packard, 2005.
9 Packard, 2005, p. 12.
10 Schatz, 1981, p. 58.
11 Buscombe and Pearson, 1998, p. 3.
12 This debate would continue in the years following *Brokeback Mountain* and would again be tied to a Focus Features production. *Milk*'s rather timely release coincided with one of the most intense periods of gay and lesbian activism to challenge the anti-gay marriage protection bill known as Proposition 8. Upon winning the award for Best Screenplay at the 2008 Academy Awards, Dustin Lance Black made an explicit note of the issue.
13 Kitses, 2007, p. 23.

14 The original independent Westerns of the 1940s and 1950s were a different matter and functioned solely as low-budget quick-return genre pictures. These older independently produced Western are historically associated with the B-picture production context coming from the poverty row studios. See Tzioumakis, 2006, pp. 63–97.

15 Bazin, 1971 [1953].

16 Wood, 1968; Kitses, 1969.

17 Cawelti, 1971; Wright, 1975.

18 Lévi-Strauss, 1968.

19 Kitses, 1969, p. 11.

20 Kitses, 1969, p. 11.

21 Kitses, 1969, p. 17.

22 Kitses's move seems to anticipate the ideological shift from structural to post-structural modes of thinking since the book was published on the cusp of transformation in the late 1960s.

23 Cawelti, 1971, p. 67.

24 Cawelti, 1971, p. 113.

25 I have not discussed *Six-Guns and Society* here since it adds little to what has already been said.

26 Eleftheriotis, 2001, pp. 92–133.

27 Two other contemporary Westerns, *The Hi-Low Country* and *All The Pretty Horses* (Billy Bob Thornton, 2000) are also set in the 1960s.

28 Sedgwick, 1990.

29 Sedgwick, 1990, p. 11.

30 Proulx, 2005, p. 131.

31 Kitses, 2007, p. 25.

32 Halberstam, 2005, pp. 36–7.

33 There are a number of gay and lesbian texts that tell the story of middle-aged protagonists who move from the city back to the country. These are less a challenge to metronormativity than carriers of a conservative impulse in which the family offers the happiness and solace that queer urbanity reneges. The two examples I am thinking of here are the films *Big Eden* (Bezucha, 2000), in which a successful New York artists returns home to Montana and falls in love with home cooking and a Native American, and Ellen DeGeneres's short-lived sitcom *The Ellen Show* (CBS 2001–2), in which she escapes the stress of city living to go and live with her family in a small town.

34 The 'fishing trips' are also reminiscent of the fishing pretence and secret identity in the Rock Hudson vehicle *A Man's Favourite Sport* (Hawks,

1963). In the film Hudson pretends to be a fishing expert but the secret is that he has never been fishing. This is another of the many films in which Hudson was positioned in relation to a secret about his identity.

35 Calhoun, 2006, p. 60.
36 Anon., *Interview*, 2006.
37 Cawelti, 1971, p. 68.
38 Calhoun, 2006, p. 62.
39 Cawelti, 1971, p. 76.
40 Tompkins, 1992, p. 4.
41 Tompkins, 1992, p. 39.
42 Doane, 1987, pp. 106–7.
43 Neale, 1983, p. 7.
44 Cawelti, 1971, p. 89.
45 Tompkins, 1992, p. 51.
46 Villarejo, 2006.
47 Tompkins, 1992, p. 66.
48 Sedgwick, 1990, p. 3.
49 The subject of silence and its relationship to homosexuality and queerness has been explored by both Jonathan Katz (1999) and Glyn Davis (2008). Katz writes about John Cage and suggests a reading of Cage's musical silences as 'a chosen mode of resistance'. Glyn Davis suggests that television's use of sound in relation to sexuality opens up a space to consider it a form of queerness.
50 Airdate 13/10/2005.
51 For example, Cohan, 1997; White, 1999; Farmer, 2000; Lang, 2002.
52 In *Between Men: English Literature and Male Homosocial Desire*, Sedgwick suggests that the continuum between male homosociality and male homosexuality is ruptured in the nineteenth century. Homophobia and misogyny become a means to keep the homosocial and the homosexual as discontinuous; Sedgwick, 1985.
53 Russo, 1987, p. 81.
54 Ellis Hanson lays this debate out in more detail in the introduction of *Out Takes: Essays on Queer Theory and Film* (1999).
55 Merck, 1980; Halberstam, 1998; White, 1999; Savoy, 1999.
56 Interestingly, though, Brett Farmer does recount a majority gay audience at a screening of *Red River* (2000, p. 277 n.80).
57 Pye, 1996, p. 16.
58 White, 1999, p. 197.
59 Doty, 1993.

60 Ingraham, 2004, p. 1.
61 White, 1999.
62 Miller, 1991, p. 124.
63 Creekmur, 1995; Cohan, 1997; Lang, 2002.
64 Dyer, 2002, p. 3.
65 Cawelti, 1971, p. 72.
66 Lang, 2002, p. 93.
67 Miller, 1991, p. 125.
68 Waugh, 2006, p. 42.
69 Cohan, 1997, p. 216.
70 Cohan, 1997, p. 203.
71 Cohan, 1997, pp. 203–5.
72 Farmer, 2000, p. 224.
73 Cohan, 1997, p. 212.
74 The dialogue was transcribed from the DVD version of the film (*Red River*, MGM Home Entertainment, 2007, Region 2).
75 Wood, 2003, p. 72.
76 Cohan, 1997, p. 213.
77 Wood, 2003.
78 Miller, 1991; Edelman, 1999; Miller, 1999.
79 Jensen, 2007 (accessed 15 July 2008).
80 Bersani, 1996.
81 As if to emphasise the Freudian overtones of this 'taking from behind' the scene is witnessed by Dan Evans's son, thus staging the whole shoot-out scenario as a primal scene. In Freud's case study of the Wolf Man the patient's primal scene is recounted through his witnessing of his father penetrating his mother from behind as *coitus a tergo*; Freud, 1991.
82 Two articles on *Brokeback Mountain* actually use the word 'lonesome' in their titles as a reference to Warhol's *Lonesome Cowboys*: Clarke, 2006; Osterweil, 2007.
83 Meyer, 2002, p. 150.
84 A reproduction of this page can be found in *Andy Warhol 'Giant Size'*, 2006, p. 58, and Meyer, 2002, p. 119.
85 My analysis of *Horse* is based on having seen the film on two occasions, both in exhibition contexts. This is supplemented by Ronald Tavel's script and notes.
86 They were played by Tosh Carillo, Larry Latreille, Dan Cassidy and film critic Gregory Battock.
87 Tavel, 1965.

88 Watson, 2003, pp. 367–1; Meyer, 2002, pp. 153–6.
89 Waugh, 1996; Tinkcom, 2002, pp. 110–13; Dyer, 2003, pp. 157–9.
90 Watson, 2004, p. 369.
91 Warhol and Hackett, 1990, p. 261.
92 Watson, 2003, p. 371.
93 Warhol and Hackett, 1990, p. 261–2.
94 Tinkcom, 2002, p. 110.
95 Dyer, 2003, p. 158.
96 Gidal, 1971, p. 130.
97 Dyer, 2003, pp. 157–9.
98 Tinkcom, 2002, p. 110.
99 Dyer, 2003, pp. 158–9.
100 Tinkcom, 2002, p. 111.
101 For an account of Bob Mizer and the postwar physique culture see Waugh, 1996, pp. 215–83.
102 Stevenson, 1997, p. 26.
103 Nealon, 2001, pp. 99–139.
104 Nealon, 2001, p. 100.
105 Charles Musser disagrees with the claim that *The Great Train Robbery* is the first movie Western. Instead, he argues that *The Great Train Robbery* more accurately belongs to the travel genre. The film's categorisation is retrospectively a Western but the initial reception of the film would have viewed it in relation to the travel genre; Musser, 1984.
106 Dyer, 2002, pp. 122–8.
107 Waugh, 1996, p. 228.

Chapter 3

1 Ahmed, 2004, pp. 2–3.
2 Love, 2007, p. 32.
3 Brooks, 1995.
4 For comprehensive overviews and key writings on film melodrama see Gledhill, 1987; Landy 1991; Singer 2001.
5 For an examination of this convention see Doane, 1987.
6 See Neale, 1986.
7 Kitses, 2007, pp. 22–7; Osterweil, 2007, pp. 38–43.
8 Osterweil, 2007, p. 38.
9 Love, 2007.
10 Love, 2007, p. 147.

11 Love, 2007, p. 146.
12 Williams, 2001, p. 36; Gledhill, 1987, p. 32.
13 Doane, 1987, p. 98.
14 Elsaesser, 1987, p. 50.
15 The concept of it being too late and temporal irreversibility is analysed in Neale, 1986.
16 Foucault, 1998.
17 Dyer, 2002, pp. 46–8.
18 Doane, 1987, p.76.
19 Ibid. p. 76.
20 Ibid. p. 90.
21 Ibid. p. 112.
22 Sedgwick, 1990.
23 Bersani, 1988.
24 Bersani, 1999, p. 4.
25 Bersani, 1988, p. 212.
26 Halberstam, 2008, p. 140; Edelman, 2005; Love, 2007.
27 Halberstam, 2008, p. 150.
28 Nowell-Smith, 1977, p. 115.

Chapter 4

1 Mulvey, 1975.
2 Edelman, 1999, p. 72.
3 Baudry, 1974; Metz, 1975; Mulvey, 1975.
4 Mayne, 1993, p. 37.
5 Mayne, 1993, p. 37.
6 Spivak, 1994.
7 Dyer, 1977. There are publications which precede this on the topic of homosexuality and the cinema but they are written from a veiled position in which the author's homosexuality remains encoded. A good example of this is Parker Tyler's *Screening the Sexes: Homosexuality in the Movies*, 1972.
8 For an excellent account of the lesbian history see White, 1999.
9 For accounts of this aspect of gay spectatorship see Dyer, 1986; Staiger, 1992; Farmer, 2000; Cohan, 2005.
10 Bordwell et al., 1985, p. 208.
11 Bech, 1997, p. 105.
12 Bech, 1997, p. 106.

13 Bowser, 1994, p. 57.
14 Bowser, 1994, pp. 57–8.
15 Bowser, 1994, p. 58.
16 Thompson in Bordwell et al., 1985, pp. 209–10.
17 Thompson in Bordwell et al., 1985, p. 209.
18 Salt, 1977, p. 52.
19 Mulvey, 1975.
20 Bech, 1997, p. 107.
21 Gove, 2000, p. 140.
22 Gove, 2000, p. 140.
23 Silverstein and Picano, 2004, p. 55.
24 Houlbrook, 2005, pp. 56–9.
25 Houlbrook, 2005, p. 59.
26 Brasell, 1992; de Villiers, 2007; Kooijman, 2009.
27 Brasell, 1992, p. 63.
28 Brasell, 1992, p. 63.
29 Brasell, 1992, p. 60.
30 de Villiers, 2007 (accessed 16 May 2009).
31 Metz, 1975, pp. 48–50.
32 The exception here would be Slavoj Zizek. His 'back to the suture' resurrected the concept offering a useful explanation of its application in cinema. His chapter is also a deliberate baiting of the post-theory project that Zizek obviously views as antagonistic to his own film theory project; Zizek, 2001.
33 Miller, 1977/78; Oudart, 1977/78.
34 Heath, 1981, p. 88.
35 Heath, 1981, p. 89.
36 The symbolic order in Lacanian psychoanalysis is understood as the realm of language, law and culture. The symbolic gives us meaning because we are able to make sense of ourselves as subjects through the tangibility of cultural 'things' like speech and signification.
37 Dayan, 1976, p. 445.
38 Dayan, 1976, p. 439.
39 The temporally asynchronous structure of these shots of looking backward to 1963 and presently to 1981 can be read as an instance of queer temporality. In queer studies the recent turn to time and temporality works from the assumption that categories of normative time are only natural for those who are privileged by them. The concept of queer temporality offers alternatives to, and makes visible, normative time;

literally and figuratively normative time is straight time in that its basic structuring principle is linearity, continuity and progression which this scene briefly eschews in its collapsing of timeframes. Queerness can be understood as a challenge to the principles of normative time and conventional temporally linear editing patterns simply because being queer is experientially outside those definitions of what constitutes a normative temporality. Queer time is desire reconfigured to embrace temporal displacements, especially with regard to the past and the future. Queer time's refusal of normative time and linear logic in editing instead favours differences of temporal experience: asynchrony, discontinuity, belatedness, arrest, coincidence, time wasting, reversal, time-travel, the palimpsest, boredom and ennui. These are means of negotiating queerness in relation to the experience of time and ultimately impact upon the desire for alternative histories and futures.

40 Love, 2007.
41 Miller, 2007, p. 56.
42 Miller, 2007, p. 58.
43 Thanks to Lydia Papadimitriou for bringing my attention to this interpretation.
44 Browne, 1975. Nick Browne also revisits this important article a few years later in Browne, 1977.

Bibliography

Ahmed, Sara (2004), *The Cultural Politics of Emotion*, Edinburgh: Edinburgh University Press.

Albert, Anita (2000), 'Finally, a movie comes in under budget', *Los Angeles Business Journal*, 11 December 2000; 22(50).

Anon. (2003), 'Universal's independent movie operation combines U.S. distribution, foreign sales,' *Deal Memo*, May 2003; 10(9):10.

Anon. (2006), *Interview*, March 2006, pp. 210–21.

Anon. (2006), *Andy Warhol 'Giant Size'*, London and New York: Phaidon.

Baudry, Jean-Louis (1974), 'Ideological effects of the basic cinematographic apparatus', *Film Quarterly* 1974; 28(2):39–47.

Bazin, André (1971 [1953]), 'The Western: or the American film *par excellence*', in *What is Cinema?*, vol. 2, Berkeley: University of California Press, pp. 149–57.

Bech, Henning (1997), *When Men Meet: Homosexuality and Modernity*, Cambridge: Polity Press.

Benshoff, Harry M. (2008), 'Brokering *Brokeback Mountain* – a local reception study', *Jump Cut*, Spring 2008; no. 50. Online: http://www.ejumpcut.org/archive/jc50.2008/BrokbkMtn/index.html (accessed 10 January 2010)

Berlant, Lauren (2008), *The Female Complaint: The Unfinished Business of Sentimentality in American Culture*, Durham: Duke University Press.

Bersani, Leo (1988), 'Is the rectum a grave?', in Douglas Crimp (ed.) *AIDS: Cultural Analysis/Cultural Activism*, Massachusetts: MIT Press.

Bersani, Leo (1996), *Homos*, New York: Harvard University Press.

Bersani, Leo (1999), *The Culture of Redemption*, New York: Universe Press.

Bordwell, David, Janet Staiger and Kristin Thompson (1985), *The Classical Hollywood Cinema: Film Style and Mode of Production to 1960*, New York: Routledge and Kegan Paul.

Bowser, Eileen (1994), *The Transformation of Cinema, 1907–1915*, History of American Cinema, vol. 2, Berkeley: University of California Press.

Brasell, R. Bruce (1992), *My Hustler*: gay spectatorship and cruising', *Wide Angle* 1992; 14(2):54–64.

Brooks, Peter (1995 [1976]), *The Melodramatic Imagination*, New Haven: Yale University Press.

Browne, Nick (1975), 'The spectator-in-the-text: the rhetoric of *Stagecoach*', *Film Quarterly* 1975; 29(2):26–38.

Browne, Nick (1977), 'Narrative point of view: the rhetoric of *Au Hasard Balthazar*', *Film Quarterly* 1977; 31(1):19–31.

Buscombe, Ed and Roberta Pearson (eds.) (1998), *Back in the Saddle Again: New Essays on the Western*, London: BFI.

Calhoun, John (2006), 'Peaks and valleys', *American Cinematographer* 2006; 87(1):58–67.

Cawelti, John G. (1971 [1984]), *The Six-Gun Mystique*, Ohio: Bowling Green State University Press.

Clarke, Roger (2006), 'Lonesome cowboys', *Sight and Sound*, January 2006, pp. 28–32.

Cohan, Steve (1997), *Masked Men: Masculinity and the Movies in the Fifties*, New York and London: Routledge.

Cohan, Steve (2005), *Incongruous Entertainment: Camp, Cultural Value, and the MGM Musical*, Durham: Duke University Press.

Creekmur, Corey K. (1995), 'Acting like a man: masculine performance in *My Darling Clementine*', in Corey K. Creekmur and Alexander Doty (eds) *Out in Culture: Gay, Lesbian, and Queer Essays on Popular Culture*, Durham: Duke University Press, pp. 167–82.

Crothers Dilley, Whitney (2007), *The Cinema of Ang Lee: The Other Side of the Screen*, London: Wallflower Press.

Cvetkovich, Ann (2003), *An Archive of Feelings*, Durham: Duke University Press.

Davis, Glyn (2008), 'Hearing queerly: television's dissident sonics', in Glyn Davis and Gary Needham (eds) *Queer TV: Theories, Histories, Politics*, London: Routledge, pp. 172–87.

Dayan, Daniel (1976), 'The tutor-code of classical cinema', in Bill Nichols (ed.) *Movies and Methods: Volume 1*, Berkeley: University of California Press, pp. 438–51.

de Villiers, Nicholas (2007), 'Glancing, cruising, staring: queer ways of looking', *Bright Lights Film Journal* 2007, no. 57. Online: http://www.brightlightsfilm.com/57/queer.html (accessed 10 January 2010).

Doane, Mary Ann (1987), *The Desire to Desire: The Woman's Film of the 1940s*, Bloomington and Indianapolis: Indiana University Press.

Doty, Alexander (1993), *Making Things Perfectly Queer: Interpreting Mass Culture*, Minneapolis: University of Minnesota Press.

Dunkley, Cathy and Jonathan Bing (2002), *Daily Variety*, 4 December 2002, p. 35.

Dyer, Richard (ed.) (1977), *Gay and Film*, London: British Film Institute.

Dyer, Richard (1986), *Heavenly Bodies: Film Stars and Society*, London: Macmillan.

Richard Dyer (2002), 'Don't look now: the instabilities of the male pin-up', in *Only Entertainment*, London: Routledge, pp. 122–37.

Dyer, Richard (2002), *The Culture of Queers*, London and New York: Routledge.

Dyer, Richard (2003), *Now You See It: Studies on Lesbian and Gay Film*, 2nd edn, London: Routledge.

Edelman, Lee (1999), '*Rear Window*'s glasshole', in Ellis Hanson (ed.) *Out Takes: Essays on Queer Theory and Film*, Durham: Duke University Press, pp. 72–96.

Edelman, Lee (2005), *No Future: Queer Theory and the Death Drive*, Durham: Duke University Press.

Eleftheriotis, Dimitris (2001), *Popular Cinemas of Europe: Texts and Contexts*, New York: Continuum.

Elsaesser, Thomas (1987), 'Tales of sound and fury: observations on the family melodrama', in Christine Gledhill (ed.) *Home is Where the Heart Is: Studies in Melodrama and the Woman's Film*, London: BFI, pp. 43–69.

Farmer, Brett (2000), *Spectacular Passions: Cinema, Fantasy, Gay Male Spectatorship*, Durham: Duke University Press.

Foucault, Michel (1998), *The History of Sexuality, Vol. 1: The Will to Knowledge*, London: Penguin.

Freud, Sigmund (1991), *Case Histories: Ratman, Schreber, Wolf Man, Case of Female Homosexuality*, London: Penguin.

Gidal, Peter (1971), *Andy Warhol: Films and Paintings*, Studio Vista: London.

Gledhill, Christine (ed.) (1987), *Home is Where the Heart Is: Studies in Melodrama and the Woman's Film*, London: BFI.

Gove, Ben (2000), *Cruising Culture: Promiscuity, Desire and American Gay Literature*, Edinburgh: Edinburgh University Press.

Halberstam, Judith (1998), *Female Masculinity*, Durham: Duke University Press.

Halberstam, Judith (2005), *In a Queer Time and Place: Transgender Bodies, Subcultural Lives*, New York: New York University Press.

Halberstam, Judith (2008), 'The anti-social turn in queer studies', *Graduate Journal of Social Science* 2008, 5(2):140–56.

Hanson, Ellis (ed.) (1999), *Out Takes: Essays on Queer Theory and Film*, Durham: Duke University Press.

Harris, Dana (2000), 'Van Sant Immigrates to USA', in *Variety*, 25 September 2000, p. 28.

Heath, Stephen (1981), *Questions of Cinema*, Bloomington: Indiana University Press.

Hernandez, Greg (2005), 'Bucking the trend: gay film a test for industry', *Daily News (Los Angeles)*, 7 December 2005.

Houlbrook, Matt (2005), *Queer London: Perils and Pleasures in the Sexual Metropolis, 1918–1957*, Chicago and London: University of Chicago Press.

Ingraham, Chrys (2004) (ed.), *Thinking Straight: The Power, The Promise, and the Paradox of Heterosexuality*, New York and London: Routledge.

Jensen, Michael (2007), Review of Russell Crowe's '3:10 to Yuma'. Online: http://www.afterelton.com/movies/2007/9/310toyuma (accessed 13 October 2009)

Katz, Jonathan (1999), 'John Cage's queer silence; or how to avoid making matters worse', *GLQ: Journal of Gay and Lesbian Studies* 1999; 5(2):231–52.

King, Geoff (2009), *Indiewood USA . . . Where Hollywood Meets Independent Cinema*', London: I. B Tauris.

Kitses, Jim (1969), *Horizons West*, London: Thames and Hudson & British Film Institute.

Kitses, Jim (2007), 'All that Brokeback allows', in *Film Quarterly* 2007; 60(3):22–7.

Kooijman, Jaap (2009), 'Cruising the channels: the queerness of zapping', in Glyn Davis and Gary Needham (eds) *Queer TV: Theories, Histories, Politics*, London: Routledge, pp. 159–71.

Kupelian, David (2007), '*Brokeback Mountain*: rape of the Marlboro Man'. Online: http://www.worldnetdaily.com/news/article.asp?ARTICLE_ID=48076 (accessed 13 October 2009)

Landy, Marcia (ed.) (1991), *Imitations of Life: A Reader on Film and Television Melodrama*, Detroit: Wayne State University Press.

Lang, Robert (2002), *Masculine Interests: Homoerotics in Hollywood Film*, New York: Columbia University Press.

Lang, Kirsty (2005), 'It's not a gay cowboy movie', *Independent*, 16 December 2005.

Lévi-Strauss, Claude (1968), *Structural Anthropology*, London: Allen Lane.

Love, Heather (2007), *Feeling Backward: Loss and the Politics of Queer History*, Cambridge and London: Harvard University Press.

Lyons, Charles (2000), 'United slates of USA', *Variety*, 14 February 2000.

Lyons, Charles (2001), 'USA Films hopes 'Traffic' will jam', *Variety*, 15 January 2001, p. 4.

Lyons, Charles (2002), 'U Speciality arms to link under one label', *Variety*, 7 January 2002, p. 6.

McClintock, Pamela (2006), 'Quaid quits "cowboy" suit', *Daily Variety*, 3 May 2006, p. 1.

Mayne, Judith (1993), *Cinema and Spectatorship*, London and New York: Routledge.

Merck, Mandy (1980), 'Travesty on the old frontier', Jane Clark and Diana Simmonds (eds) *Move Over Misconceptions: Doris Day Reappraised*, London: British Film Institute, pp. 21–8.

Metz, Christian (1975), 'The imaginary signifier', *Screen* 1975; 16(2):14–76.

Meyer, Richard (2002), *Outlaw Representation: Censorship and Homosexuality in Twentieth-Century American Art*, Boston: Beacon Press.

Miller, Jacques-Alain (1977/78), 'Suture', *Screen* 1977/78; 18(4):24–34.

Miller, D. A. (1991), 'Anal *Rope*', in Diana Fuss (ed.) *Inside/Out: Lesbian Theories, Gay Theories*, London and New York: Routledge, pp. 119–41.

Miller, D. A. (1999), 'Visual pleasure in 1959', in Hanson, Ellis (ed.) *Out Takes: Essays on Queer Theory and Film*, Durham: Duke University Press, pp. 97–125.

Miller, D. A. (2007), 'On the universality of *Brokeback Mountain*', *Film Quarterly* 2007, 60(3):50–61.

Mulvey, Laura (1975), 'Visual pleasure and narrative cinema', *Screen* 1975; 16(3):6–18.

Musser, Charles (1984), 'The travel genre in 1903–04: moving toward fictional narratives', *Iris* 1984; 2(1):24–52.

Neale, Steve (1983), 'Masculinity as spectacle: reflections on men and mainstream cinema', *Screen* 1983; 24(6):2–16.

Neale, Steve (1986), 'Melodrama and tears', *Screen* 1986; 27(6):6–22.

Nealon, Christopher (2001), *Foundlings: Lesbian and Gay Historical Emotion Before Stonewall*, Durham: Duke University Press.

Nowell-Smith, Geoffrey (1977), 'Dossier on Melodrama', *Screen* 1977; 18(2):105–19.

Osterweil, Ara (2007), 'Ang Lee's lonesome cowboys', *Film Quarterly* 2007; 60(3):38–42.

Oudart, Jean-Pierre (1977/78), 'Cinema and suture', *Screen* 1977/78; 18(4):35–47.

Packard, Chris (2005), *Queer Cowboys*, New York: Palgrave MacMillan.

Perren, Alisa (2009), 'Another dimension to Miramax: reassessing art and genre in the 1990s,' unpublished paper presented at the conference 'American Independent Cinema: Past, Present, Future', Liverpool John Moores University, 10 May 2009.

Proulx, Annie (2005), 'Getting movied', in *Brokeback Mountain: Story to Screenplay*, New York: Scribner, pp. 129–38.

Pye, Douglas (ed.) (1996), *The Movie Book of the Western*, London: Studio Vista.

Rich, B. Ruby (2005), 'Hello cowboy', *The Guardian*, 23 September 2005.

Rooney, David (2004a), 'Oscar indeed came into focus,' *Variety*, 1 March 2004, p. 30.

Rooney, David (2004b), 'Focus takes rogue turn with launch of new genre arm', *Daily Variety*, 25 March 2004, p. 1.

Russo, Vito (1987), *The Celluloid Closet: Homosexuality in the Movies*, New York: Harper and Row.

Salt, Barry (1977), 'Film style and technology in the forties', *Film Quarterly* 1977; 31(1):46–57.

Savoy, Eric (1999), '"That Ain't *All* She Ain't": Doris Day and queer performativity', in Ellis Hanson (ed.) *Out Takes: Essays on Queer Theory and Film*, Durham: Duke University Press, pp. 151–82.

Schamus, James (1998), 'The rear of the back end: the economics of independent cinema', in Steve Neale and Murray Smith (eds) *Contemporary Hollywood Cinema*, London: Routledge, pp. 91–105.

Schatz, Thomas (1981), *Hollywood Genres*, Columbus: McGraw-Hill.

Sedgwick, Eve Kosofsky (1985), *Between Men: English Literature and Male Homosicial Desire*, New York: Columbia University Press.

Sedgwick, Eve Kosofsky (1990), *Epistemology of the Closet*, New York: Penguin.

Sedgwick, Eve Kosofsky (1993), 'Queer performativity: Henry James's *The Art of the Novel*', *GLQ: A Journal of Gay and Lesbian Studies* 1993; 1(1):1–16.

Silverstein, Charles and Felice Picano (2004 [1978]), *The Joy of Gay Sex*, 3rd edn, New York: Harper Collins.

Singer, Ben (2001), *Melodrama and Modernity: Early Sensational Cinema and its Contexts*, New York: Columbia University Press.

Snyder, Gabriel (2007), 'Focus looks to regain its fire,' *Variety*, 15 January 2007, p. 49.

Spivak, Gayatri Chakravorty (1994), 'In a word: interview', in Naomi Schor and Elizabeth Weed (eds) *The Essential Difference*, Indiana University Press: Bloomington and Indianapolis, pp. 151–84.

Staiger, Janet (1992), 'The logic of alternative positions: *A Star is Born*', in *Interpreting Films: Studies in the Historical Reception of American Cinema*, New Jersey: Princeton University Press, pp. 154–77.

Stevenson, Jack (1997), 'From the bedroom to the Bijou: a secret history of gay sex cinema', *Film Quarterly* 1997, 51(1):24–31.

Tavel, Ronald (1965), *Horse*, film script.

Tinkcom, Matthew (2002), *Working Like a Homosexual: Camp, Capital, Cinema*, Durham, Duke University Press.

Tyler, Parker (1972), *Screening the Sexes: Homosexuality in the Movies*, New York: Holt, Reinhart and Winston.

Tzioumakis, Yannis (2006), *American Independent Cinema: An Introduction*, Edinburgh University Press, Edinburgh.

Tzioumakis, Yannis (2009a), 'After the independent, the indie and indiewood: the (ever)changing discourse of American independent cinema', unpublished paper presented at the conference 'What is Film? Change and Continuity in the Twenty-First Century', Portland, Oregon, 7 November 2009.

Tzioumakis, Yannis (2009b), *The Spanish Prisoner*, Edinburgh: Edinburgh University Press.

Vachon, Christine (2006), *A Killer Life: How an Independent Film Producer Survives Deals and Disasters in Hollywood and Beyond*, New York: Simon And Schuster.

Villarejo, Amy (2006), 'The jaws of time' [unpublished paper].

Warhol, Andy and Pat Hackett (1990), *Popism: The Warhol Sixties*, Florida: Harcourt Brace and Company.

Watson, Steve (2003), *Factory Made: Warhol and the Sixties*, Pantheon Books, New York.

Waugh, Thomas (1996), 'Cockteaser', in Jennifer Doyle, Jonathan Flatley and José Esteban Muñoz (eds) *Pop Out: Queer Warhol*, Durham: Duke University Press, pp. 51–77.

White, Patricia (1999), *Uninvited: Classical Hollywood Cinema and Lesbian Representability*, Bloomington and Indianapolis: Indiana University Press.

Williams, Linda (2001), *Playing the Race Card: Melodramas of Black and White from Uncle Tom to O. J. Simpson*, New Jersey: Princeton University Press.

Wood, Robin (1968), *Howard Hawks*, London: Thames and Hudson & British Film Institute.

Wood, Robin (2003), *Rio Bravo*, London: British Film Institute.

Wright, Will (1975), *Sixguns and Society: A Structural Study of the Western*, Berkeley: University of California Press.

Wyatt, Justin (1998), 'The formation of the 'major independent': Miramax, New Line and the New Hollywood', in Steve Neale and Murray Smith (eds) *Contemporary Hollywood Cinema*, London: Routledge, pp. 74–90.

Zizek, Slavoj (2001), *The Fright of Real Tears: Krzysztof Kieslowski Between Theory and Post-Theory*, London: BFI.

Index